A VISION EXCHANGED

An exhibition held at the Victoria & Albert Museum from 6 February until 8 April 1985 – and at the National Museum of Photography, Film and Television at Bradford from 23 April until 23 June 1985

A Vision Exchanged has been organised by the Victoria & Albert Museum, George Eastman House and the Arts Council of Great Britain

A VISION EXCHANGED
Designed by Grundy & Northedge Designers
Printed by Royle Print Limited
ISBN 0 948 107 0 57
© Text: Carolyn Bloore & Grace Seiberling
Published by the Victoria & Albert Museum

T his exhibition follows the Museum's survey, shown in 1984, *The Golden Age of British Photography 1839-1900*, and examines in detail the particularly interesting moment when the professional practice of photography crystallised out of the experiments of the Amateurs (using the term in its broadest sense) of the 1850s. Photographs of the period show a remarkable variety of colours and surfaces, embodying as they do a range of experimental methods prior to the standardisation of materials, and these need to be seen in the original. The present publication is a brief introduction to the exhibition and its main themes. The illustrations cover the important subjects into which the period sub-divides and the catalogue provides a great deal of valuable information. The exhibition brings to light many forgotten photographers and works found in a wide variety of collections by its organisers: Carolyn Bloore in London and Professor Grace Seiberling in Rochester, New York. Their joint work will be published in book form, under the same title as this catalogue, later in 1985 by the University of Chicago Press. The exhibition was first shown at the International Museum of Photography at George Eastman House, Rochester, N.Y., and we are grateful to our American colleagues for their part in its organisation. Much of the burden of organisation has also been borne by The Arts Council of Great Britain, which helped foster the idea of the exhibition some years ago through its Photography committee. The Museum adds its warmest thanks to the many lenders and helpers whose names appear elsewhere in the catalogue.

C.M. Kauffmann
Keeper of Prints and Drawings & Photographs
Mark Haworth-Booth
Assistant Keeper of Photographs

I n England in 1850 photography was a curiosity and a marvel. By 1860 it was widely known and accepted as a means of recording information and making pictures. In the decade between these two dates a remarkable group of photographers practiced this new medium, which they considered an "art-science". They provided the larger public with more reliable processes, institutions to spread knowledge about photography, and ideas about the appropriate subject matter and compositional types for photographs.

They were amateurs in the broadest sense of the word – men and women with liberal educations who approached a variety of activities with ease and confidence. They were as likely to be acquainted with art, through their practice of sketching and their collections of prints, as they were to be engaged in the study of natural history or other branches of science.

They practiced photography in a particular social context, and it was natural for them to form organizations modelled on the learned societies and dining clubs to which they belonged. The photographs in this exhibition were made by members of the Photographic Exchange Club (1855-1858) and by those who participated in exchanges of prints within the Photographic Society of London (now the Royal Photographic Society).

They had a vision of photography as an art/science, and as an activity which encompassed their diverse interests. By making photographs which resembled the pictures they knew, they included photography in the arts and helped to legitimize the medium. The scientific side of photography interested them as well; experimenting with its chemistry was part of the challenge of the new medium.

Amateurs of the 1850s had a vision of photography as the continuation of a pictorial tradition. Their choices of picturesque subjects and artistic compositions can still be recognized in many pictures today – even postcards. Their 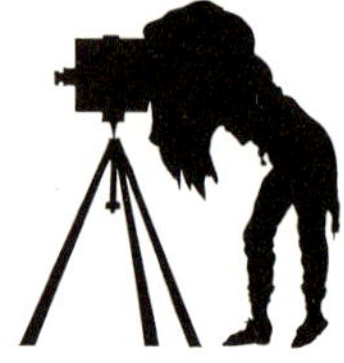 vision of photography as an art/science was exchanged, during the course of the 1850s, for another one that was more commercially oriented and less connected with a particular class and its ideals.

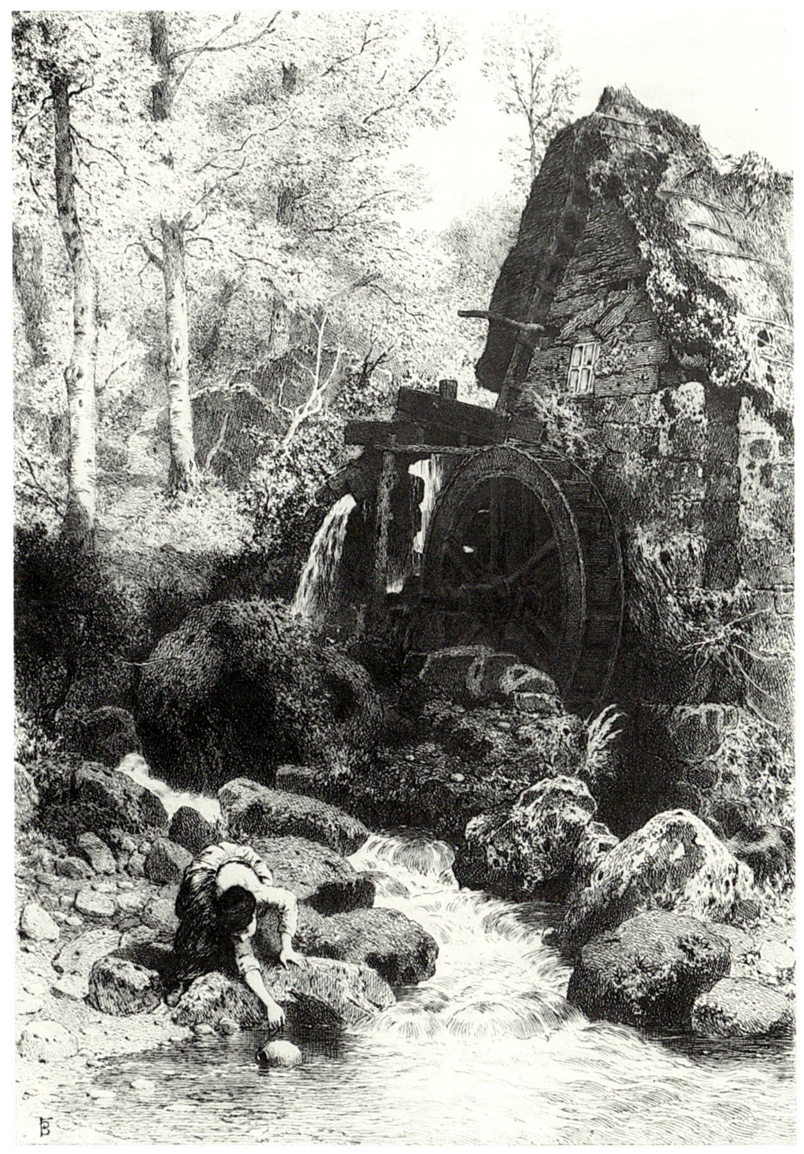

E arly photographers thought of photographs as pictures. They had grown up with copies of works of art and engravings and lithographs of English and foreign scenery. Books like Westall's *Landscape Album* (1832) were often used to teach drawing. When photographers started making pictures with cameras, they had models in their heads of what to take and how to compose it. They assembled their pictures in albums like those which they had previously used to collect sketches, prints, watercolours, mementos and inscriptions from friends.

When Thereza Llewelyn made an album of photograms of seaweed, she was doing something which was at once scientific and aesthetic. She recorded the botanical names of her specimens but, like the women who arranged seaweeds in sentiment or remembrance albums, she made them into attractive patterns.

Thomas Eaton, like many of his colleagues, was an amateur artist. When he began photographing in the 1840s, he assembled an album of "camera sketches" instead of the pencil or watercolour sketches he must have made in other albums.

A n anonymous review of the first exhibition of photographs at the Society of Arts in 1852 characterized the subject matter of the British photographs:

"The English are, for the most part, representations of the peaceful village; the unassuming church, among its tombstones and trees; the gnarled oak, standing alone in the forest; intricate masses of tangled wood, reflected in some dark pool; shocks of corn, drooping with their weight of grain; the quiet stream with its waterlilies and rustic bridge; the wild upland pass with its foreground of crumbling rock and purple; or the still lake . . ."

A vision of England as a sort of rural paradise, as yet unaffected by the Industrial Revolution, appears in the works of amateur photographers of the 1850s. They drew upon a

151.

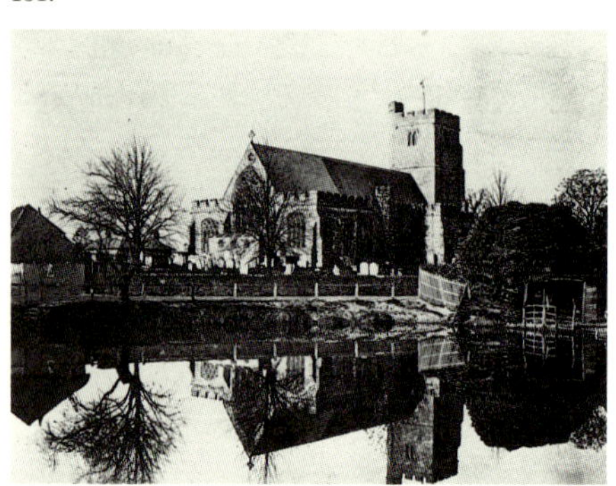

pictorial tradition for their models, and were influenced, above all, by the example of picturesque landscape.

The aesthetic category of the Picturesque included things which were neither beautiful or ugly, but which were suited for pictures because of their interesting irregularity, textures and contrasts. Eminently picturesque subjects included cottages, mills, wooded lanes, massed foliage and old trees. These appeared in the sketching manuals and books on watercolours which taught many Victorians the principles of art. P.H. Delamotte wrote several such books later in the century. William Lake Price's and H.P. Robinson's photographic manuals were based on the model of the amateur artist's manual, such as John Burnet's *Practical Treatise on Painting* (1827, many times reprinted).

2 i THE GNARLED OAK AND INTRICATE MASSSES OF TANGLED WOOD

O ld trees were considered picturesque in their decay. William Gilpin, whose *Remarks on Forest Scenery (1791)* was cited in many 19th century books on landscape and trees, wrote: "What is more beautiful, for instance, on a rugged foreground, than an old tree with a *hollow trunk?* or a *dead arm*, a *drooping bough* or a *dying branch?*"

Trees were living reminders of the past. They were often identified with famous people or events. *Herne's Oak* was mentioned in Shakespeare's *Merry Wives of Windsor*. The British Navy's demand for timbers and the early Industrial Revolution's need for wood meant that many old trees survived only in protected places. They were emblems of permanence in a period of change.

2 ii RUINED ABBEYS AND CASTLES

W hat delightful hours we passed in wandering through the quiet ruins of some venerable abbey, impressing, with wondrous truth, upon the delicate tablets we carried, the marvellous beauty of Gothic window, of broken column, and ivy wreathed arch." — James Mudd,

96.

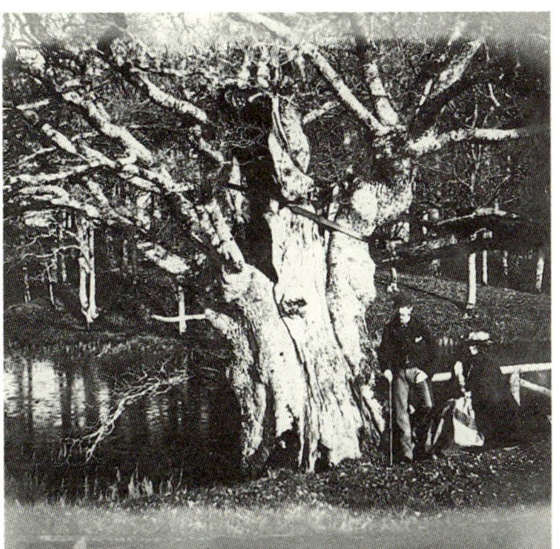

33.

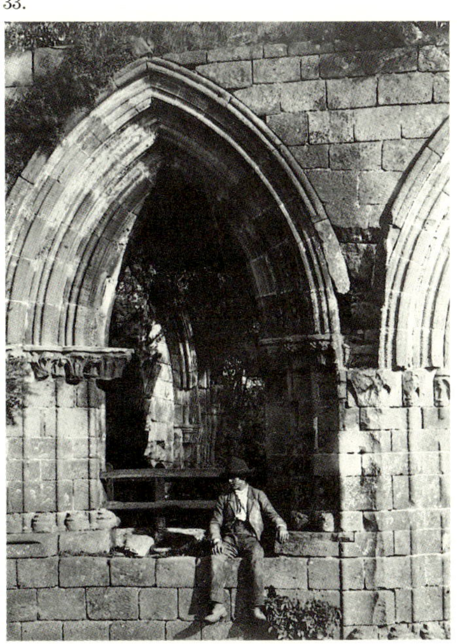

1858.

Ruins had been a favourite subject for artists of the romantic era. Amateurs of the 1850s sometimes visited them on excursions to the countryside, and many were also motivated by architectural and antiquarian as well as pictorial interests. A pride in the glories of the English past was part of the appreciation of ruins, but ruins were also reminders of the evanescence of the works of man and the way in which time and nature encroached upon them.

3 SEASHORE PHOTOGRAPHY

Sea bathing and seaside resorts were a particular delight of the Victorians. In visiting the seaside, amateur photographers looked at it in many different ways. They photographed famous monuments, like St. Michael's Mount and Conway Castle, which they knew from a century of engravings. They photographed picturesque harbours and beached boats, which were a common subject for painters and sketchers. Some, like J.D. Llewelyn, selected rocky coastal scenes which contained interesting geological features.

Because of the great amount of reflected light, seaside photography allowed short exposures. Llewelyn produced a series of "motion studies" (one of which was engraved for the *Illustrated London News*). Critics in the early 1850s complained that photography could not yet capture the motion of waves; for this reason many photographers chose to make their pictures when the tide was out.

4 GENRE SCENES

Most amateurs took family pictures. Often these were not the sort of snapshot familiar to modern photographers, but were carefully posed, though more informal than commercial portraits. At times they were derived from children's play or from the costumed tableaux and amateur theatricals which were a part of Victorian social life. They sometimes had a narrative or sentimental content similar to that of paintings of the time, which were frequently reproduced by engravings.

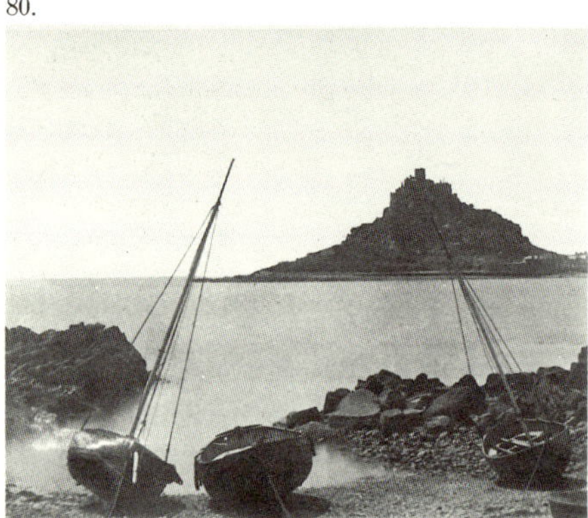

80.

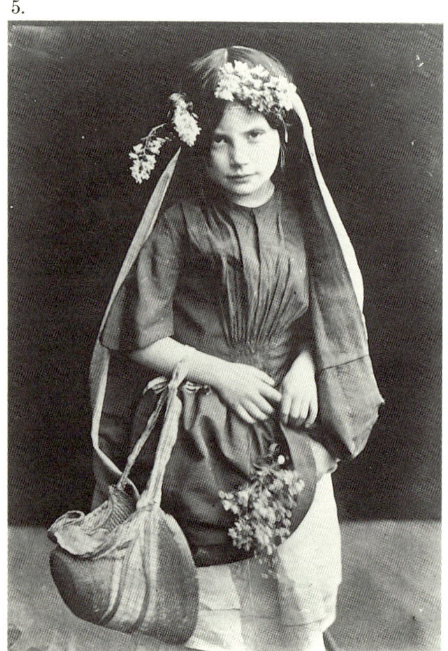

5.

In painting, the pictures showing scenes from everyday life are classified as "genre". Victorian painters like Wilkie, Mulready, W.P. Frith and others became very popular through their narrative paintings showing piquant or sentimental scenes from daily life.

Photographs of the amateurs and rising professionals intersected with the tradition of genre painting in several ways. Robert Howlett took photographs from the top of a carriage to provide William Powell Frith with figure studies for his very popular painting, *Derby Day* (1858). In some cases, like Lake Price's *Miniature*, Rejlander's *Fortune Telling*, and Lake Price's extremely popular *Don Quixote* or his stereos of *Robinson Crusoe* costumed models were posed in narrative scenes. Critics of the time saw the analogy between these photographs and paintings. Some praised the pictures as raising the level of photography as art. Others, who considered photography to be a truthful medium, were distressed by the fact that real people were posing in fictitious scenes.

81.

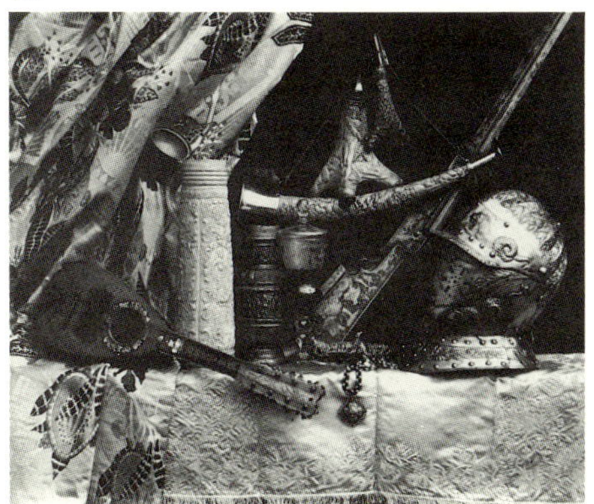

5 STILL LIFE

Still life was well established as a subject for artists. The contemporary admiration for the Dutch school of the 17th century influenced the composition and selection of objects in photographs. The photographers set up their pictures on a flat plane, with the objects arranged to look like a painting. They selected pottery, metal, brocades, fur and feathers to provide a variety of textures and surfaces. These showed off the capabilities of the camera and the skill of the photographer just as, in the past, they had demonstrated the skill of the still life painter.

Most of these pictures make reference to game or shooting. Although strict game laws had been relaxed by the mid-19th century, shooting was still an activity largely restricted to gentlemen of landed property and their friends or — in the case of F.E. Currey, who managed the Duke of Devonshire's Irish estates — their agents. Like the rare antique objects they accompany, the accoutrements of shooting are indicators of the status of these photographers.

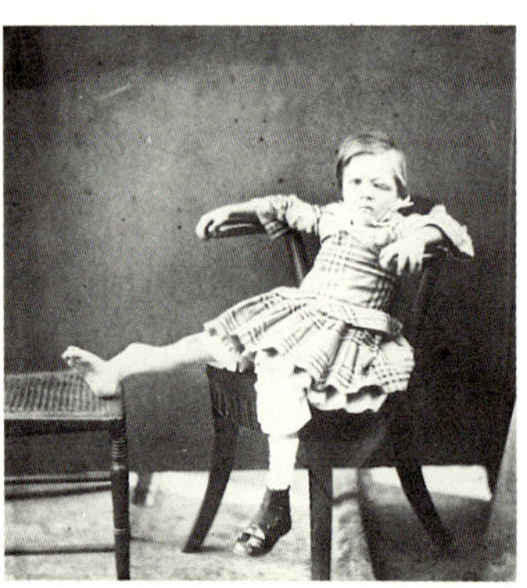

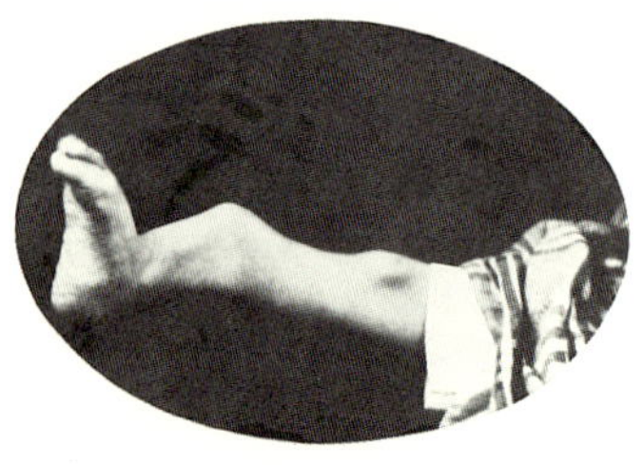

S tuffed animals and birds may not seem likely subjects for photography, but like the Count de Montizon's live animals — and Fenton's dead ones — they stem from an interest in zoology. The study of botany was very popular in the nineteenth century as well. Botanical gardens were established and the exhibition at the Crystal Palace included a selection of exotic plants. Gentlemen like Llewelyn even cultivated rare specimens in their own conservatories.

The study of natural history was intertwined with an interest in "rational leisure" which was characteristic of most classes. It could have both a scientific and an aesthetic component. Pressed seaweed and flowers arranged by young ladies in decorative patterns formed prototypes for photograms, like Thereza Llewelyn's, which were classified by their scientific names. Households sometimes had a "museum room" in which were displayed geological and antiquarian specimens, stuffed animals and birds from shooting expeditions, fossils, shells brought back from the seashore, insects and other natural curiosities.

Many early photographers had serious scientific interests, including research on the chemistry of photography. They also used photographs to record the specimens and natural phenomena which they were studying. Dr. Diamond was the first to use photography to document the insane and to use the pictures in treating his patients at the Surrey County Lunatic Asylum. Dr. Julius Pollock used photography to record deformities difficult to describe with words.

7 COPIES OF WORKS OF ART AND
ANTIQUARIAN OBJECTS

W e take it for granted that photography is a method of reproducing works of art and that such photographs are purely functional. Nineteenth century observers, accustomed to reproductive engravings, considered such photographs to be works of interpretative art. Photographic copies were potentially not only more

35.

114.

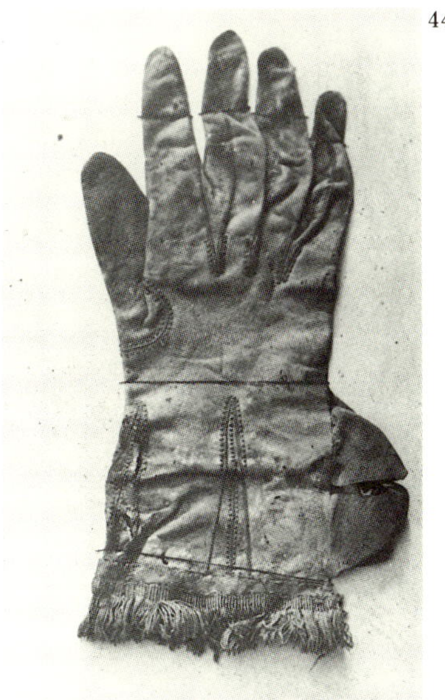

44.

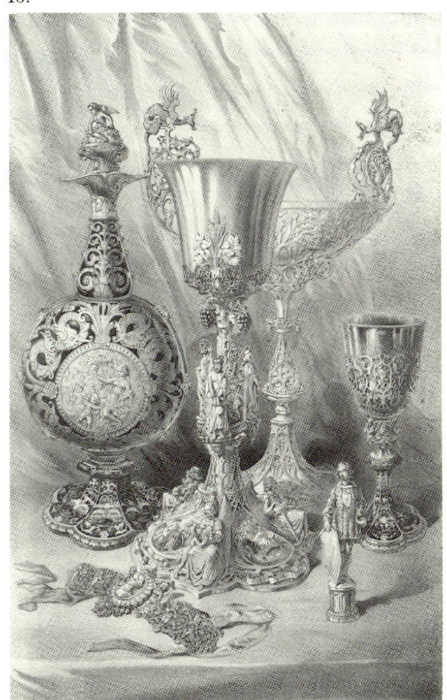

15.

accurate, but also far cheaper and less time consuming to produce than copies by traditional printmaking processes. Although early photographers foresaw the possibility of reproducing works of art, photographs did not replace the older methods until photomechanical processes became available late in the century.

8 PHOTOGRAPHY AND LITHOGRAPHY

Before they began photographing, several members of the exchange clubs were professional lithographers and artists. Francis Bedford and P.H. Delamotte were still producing lithographs during the mid-1850s. They were accomplished draughtsmen, but sometimes based their work on photographs.

Chromolithography and photography were both new techniques for reproduction at this time, and their subject matters overlapped. Both techniques were used for the reproduction of works of art and objects of vertu, sometimes, as here, in luxury publications.

Topographical lithographs or prints of objects or works of art were sometimes issued as individual prints, sometimes in sets, and sometimes in books, like Bedford's *Churches of York*. Photographers repeated many of these subjects — see Bedford's *Rievaulx Abbey* — and issued collections of photographs analogous to earlier collections of prints: Delamotte and Cundall's *A Photographic Tour Among the Abbeys of Yorkshire* (1856) and *Photographic Art Treasures* are examples.

9 EXCHANGES AND PUBLICATIONS

Apart from exhibitions, the Victorian public learned about photographs in many different ways. These included exchanges of prints, publications of photographs, presentations at learned societies or other associations and the publication of engravings after photographs.

Amateur organizations were formed for the exchange of pictures. Recipients assembled them in albums or portfolios. H.P. Robinson made a print of Guy's Cliffe, Warwickshire for each of the 21 members of the Photographic Exchange

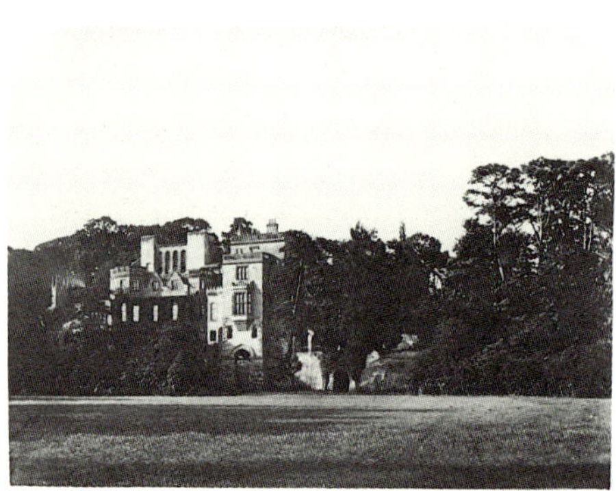

127.

160.

Club. Such exchanges enabled photographers to assemble a selection of high-quality prints, by various photographers and fostered photography within the context of an influential group of people.

'Photographic Exchange Club' albums of photographs exchanged in 1855-6 and 1857-8 are in the collections of the International Museum of Photography at George Eastman House and the Royal Photographic Society. Two similar but distinct volumes are: *The Photographic Album for the Year 1855*: *Being contributions from the Members of the Photographic Club*. London: Charles Whittingham, 1855; and *The Photographic Album for the Year 1857*: *Being contributions from the Members of the Photographic Club*. London: Charles Whittingham 1857. These are also in the collection of the Royal Photographic Society, Bath, and other collections.

Both Delamotte and Cundall took photographs of picturesque spots or noteworthy monuments within a particular area, and both published these photographs in small editions. These followed in the tradition of topographical lithographs or engravings issued in sets or books.

The preface to Cundall's *Views in Gloucestershire* stated: "These Photographic Views were taken at the request of an eminent Engineer, to be laid, in Evidence, before a committee of the House of Commons." They were developed in a post-chaise, which can be seen amidst the picturesque scenery. Cundall's pictures were meant to demonstrate the capabilities of photography as much as to document specific places.

10 EARLY PHOTOGRAPHIC PUBLICATIONS

Members of the exchange clubs participated in photographic publishing ventures as early as 1852, when the *Photographic Album* appeared, containing photographs by Fenton and Delamotte. The *Sunbeam*, which was edited by Delamotte and came out between 1857 and 1859, followed the example of the exchanges by including a variety of contributions by different photographers. Like Westall's *Landscape Album* and other topographical publications, it included information about the places shown in the photographs, often drawn from guide books or history books.

Photographic Art Treasures included a selection of prints of landscape and narrative scenes: see Lake Price's *Don Quixote* and Fenton's *Hush, Lightly Tread.* They were not photographs, but prints made by the photogalvanographic process, a relief etching process based on a photographic image. Although a costly process, it eliminated the distressing effects of fading which threatened many prints made in this decade.

Later publications no longer included such miscellanies of prints. They tended to concentrate on one type of subject matter, for example Bedford's *Pictorial Illustrations of Torquay.*

11 PRINTS BEFORE AND AFTER PHOTOGRAPHS

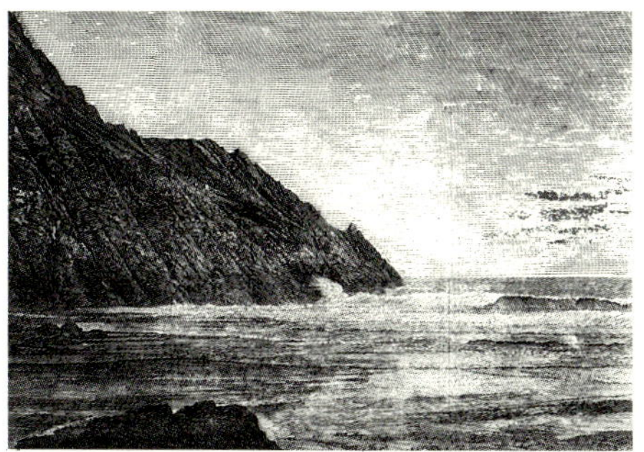

77.

As a merchant of port wine, J.J. Forrester was interested in documenting Portugal. His lithographs show the kind of visual models he had in mind when he took photographs. He turned to the new medium in part because he wanted a more accurate or convincing way of presenting something which he had already recorded in lithographs and maps — the river Douro. Despite this evidence he was unsuccessful in his attempts to convince the Portuguese and British governments to improve the river's navigability.

Llewelyn was also interested in using the capabilities of photography to show what could not be presented as successfully in other media. In a series of "motion studies" he took advantage of the speed of collodion to capture a moving steamship, and waves in Oxwich Bay. This picture was engraved for the *Illustrated London News*, an extremely popular Victorian periodical. Wood engravings after photographs introduced the new medium to a mass audience.

12 THE CHANGING LANDSCAPE

The least exploited aspect of the English landscape in photography of the 1850s was that of the new landscape wrought by industrialization and its accompanying changes. The camera, with its narrow angle of vision, was

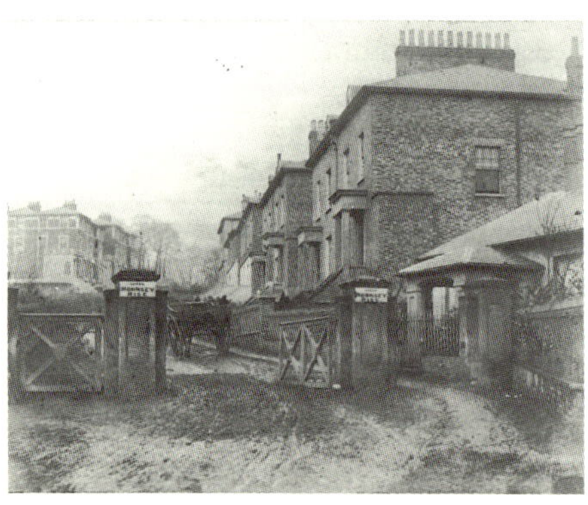

143.

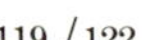119./122.

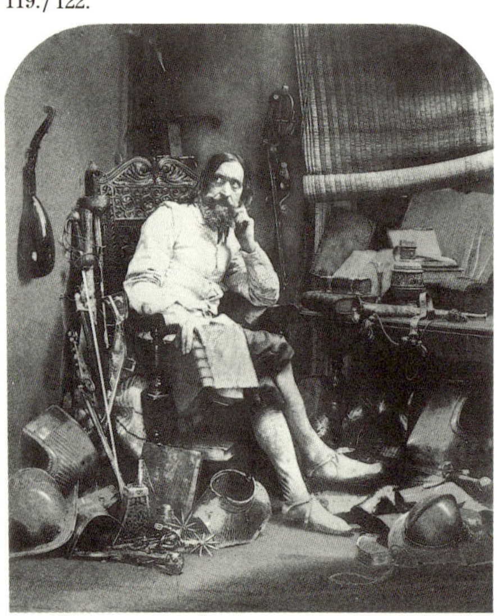

not well suited to capturing the sublime vistas which were a standard type for painters and printmakers representing subjects of the industrial revolution. Most photographers were attuned to the Picturesque, to a more intimate scale, to landscape subjects and to a view of England as stable and non-industrial.

Hornsey, where George Shadbolt lived, was soon to become a suburb of London, but he took only a few pictures which showed evidence of its expansion. Most of his photographs show its rural aspect; the only evidence of industry is handcraft.

Those photographers who chose to illustrate the structures resulting from industrialization looked at the new phenomena from the standpoint of their artistic training, seeking patterns, and organizing their pictures in conventional ways. For instance, Delamotte, in showing *Workmen in the Grounds*, uses the conventions of picturesque landscape or sees the structure of the Crystal Palace, in some pictures at least, as an abstract, decorative pattern. The most famous photographs of this type were made for publication. Delamotte's views of the reconstruction of the Crystal Palace at Sydenham and Howlett's series of the building of Brunel's steamship, *The Great Eastern*, have become well known as the first documentary photographs of engineering construction.

13 LATER PUBLICATIONS

The topographic and antiquarian traditions remained important sources for photographers and publishers. The Howitts' *Ruined Abbeys and Castles of Great Britain* was illustrated by photographs rather than engravings, but followed the model of earlier books. Publications of photographs of miscellaneous subjects were superceded by ones which presented some specific subject, often connected with travel. Bedford's *Pictorial Illustrations of Torquay and its Neighbourhood* is an example of the more specialized publications which appealed to an audience of tourists and also of the continuing importance of topography.

Robinson was extremely successful in writing manuals for the new population of photographers which began to emerge around 1860. These men and women no longer wanted detailed instructions on how to prepare materials — they could buy them ready made-up — but they appreciated Robinson's advice on how to take artistic pictures.

14 COMMERCIAL PHOTOGRAPHY

Many of the amateurs' subjects were repeated by commercial photographers in different formats. Francis Bedford was very successful in selling views of picturesque landscape and monuments. Some were sold as separate prints; in other cases they were assembled in albums. He also sold many of the same views, and many others, as stereos. He photographed subjects which amateur photographers had chosen in the 1850s: Conway Castle, harbour scenes, views in North Wales. The growth in popularity of such photographs coincided with a tremendous expansion of tourism. The railway system, the availability of Cook's Tours, other organized excursions, and the increased prosperity of the middle class in the 1850s and 1860s all meant that many more people travelled. Even those who did not, might wish to buy photographs of famous beauty spots.

Narrative scenes, especially stereos, also enjoyed a great popularity around 1860.

15 THE VISION REDEFINED

While the primary commercial market at the end of the 1850s was for portraits, there was a growing demand for topographical views. Stereo views had already become popular in the mid-1850s and were produced by the thousands in the early 1860s. Both landscape and narrative stereos could be found in nearly every middle-class household.

Photographers like Bedford, Fenton, Rejlander and Robinson adapted the kinds of photographs they had taken as amateurs and became highly successful in their professional capacity. Fenton's and Alfred Rosling's negatives, taken in the 1850s, found a larger audience when they were printed and distributed for sale by

Francis Frith in the next decade.

Robinson continued to associate with later amateurs. He and other members of the exchange clubs, such as Shadbolt and Currey, continued to make similar photographs. They belonged to a much larger amateur exchange, the Amateur Photographic Association, which was organized on a semi-commercial basis. Instead of exchanges in which each photographer contributed prints for all the others, the Association had a central store of thousands of members' negatives, which were printed at the request of the photographers and other subscribers.

By the late 1850s photography was no longer the pastime of an elite. Most of the distinguished early amateurs withdrew when the availability of photographic services and equipment put photography within the grasp of thousands of new enthusiasts. The commercial and amateur expansion of photography at the end of the 1850s was the first step for photography as a mass medium.

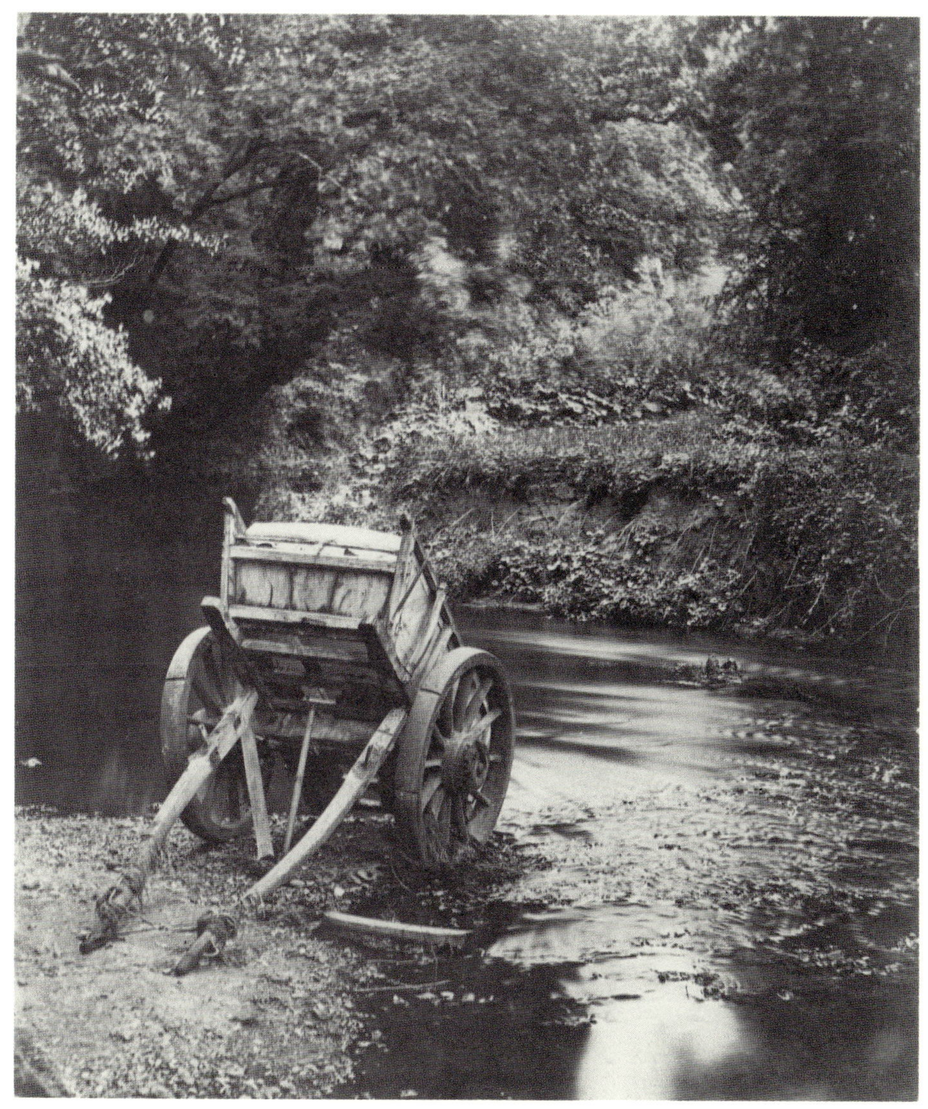

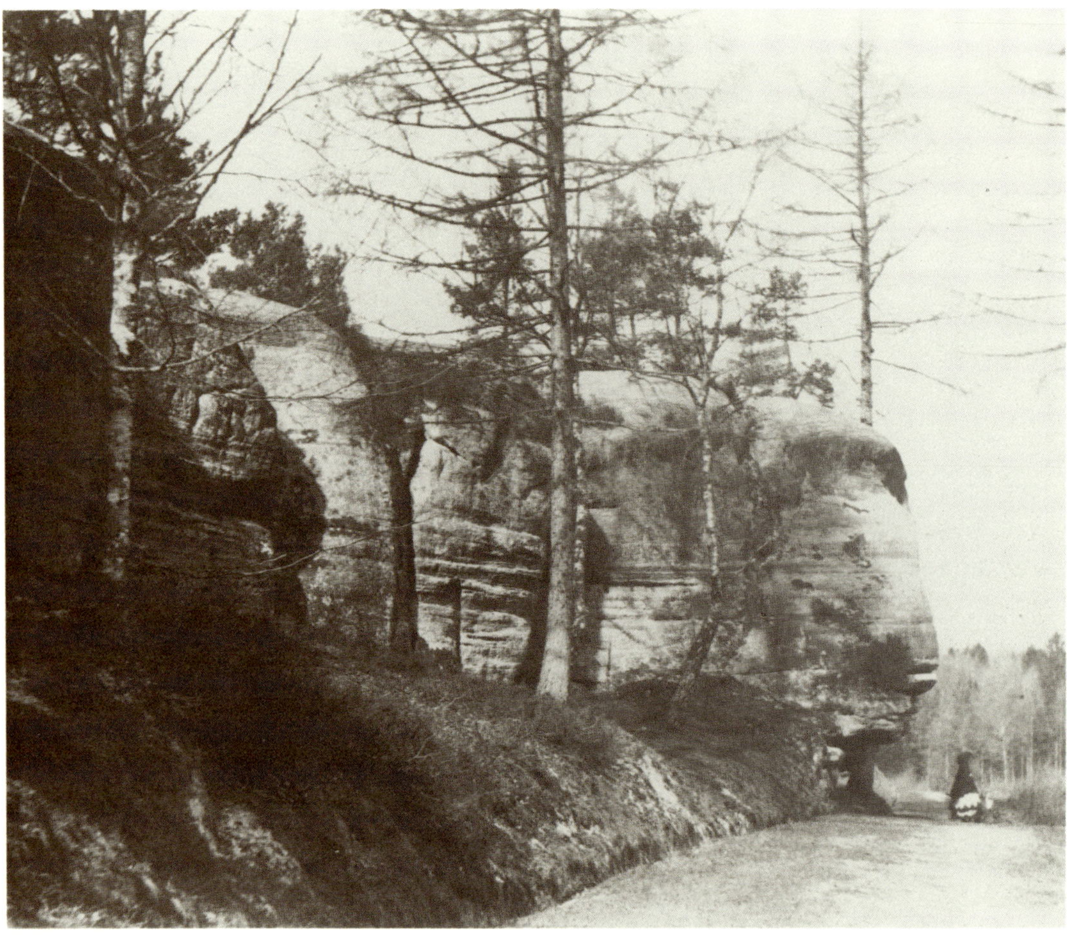

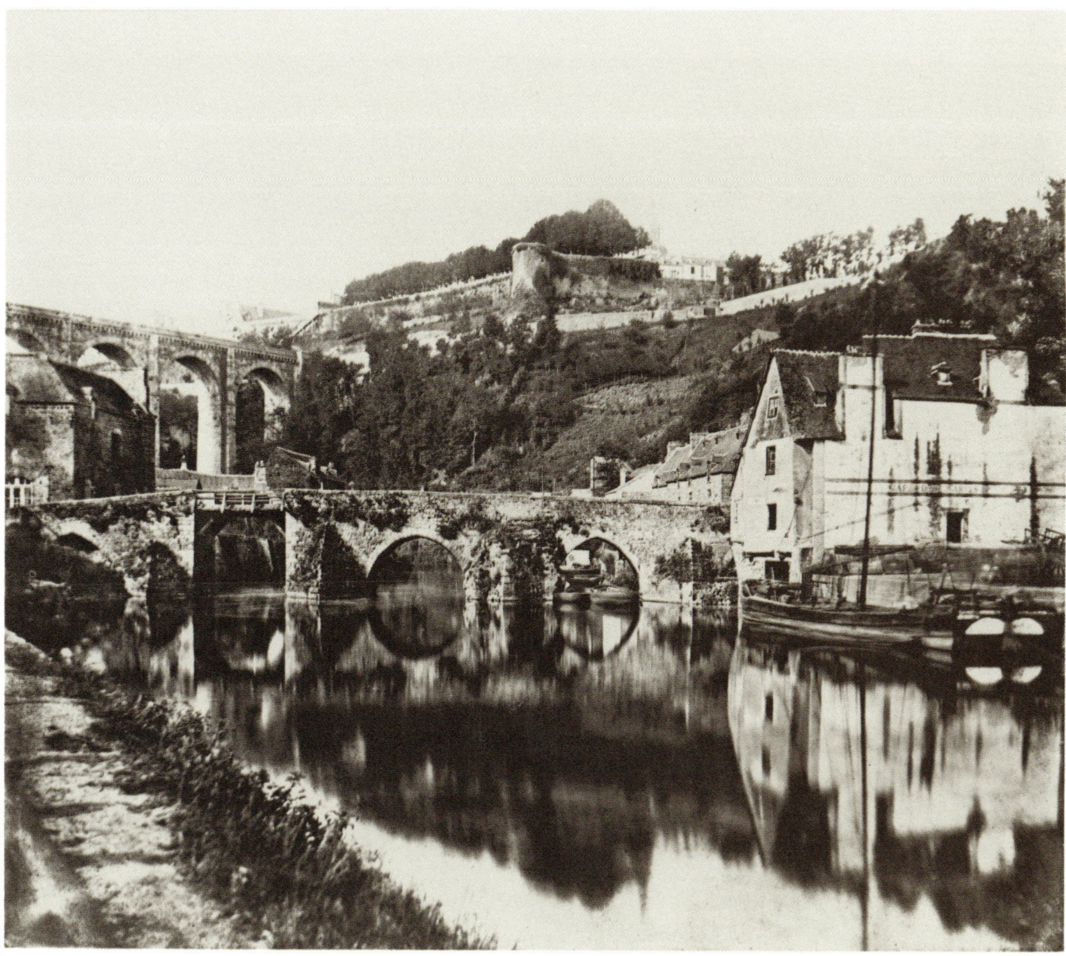

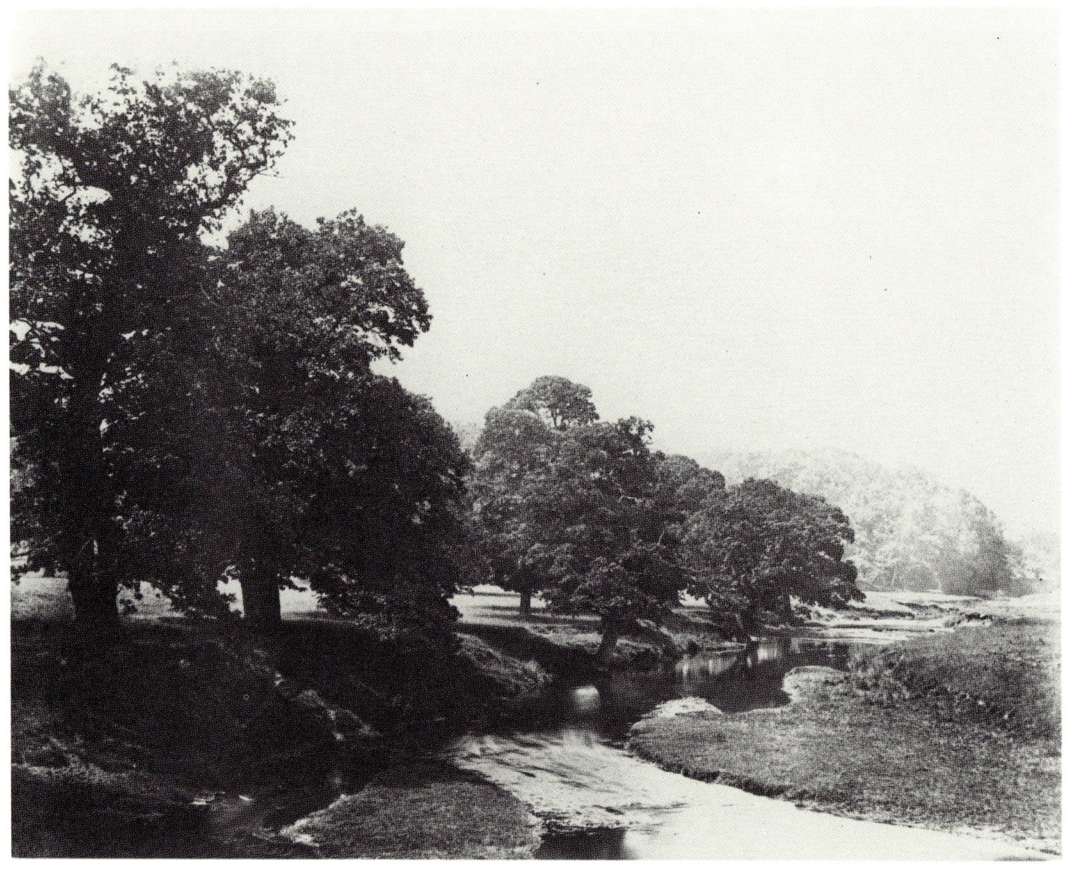

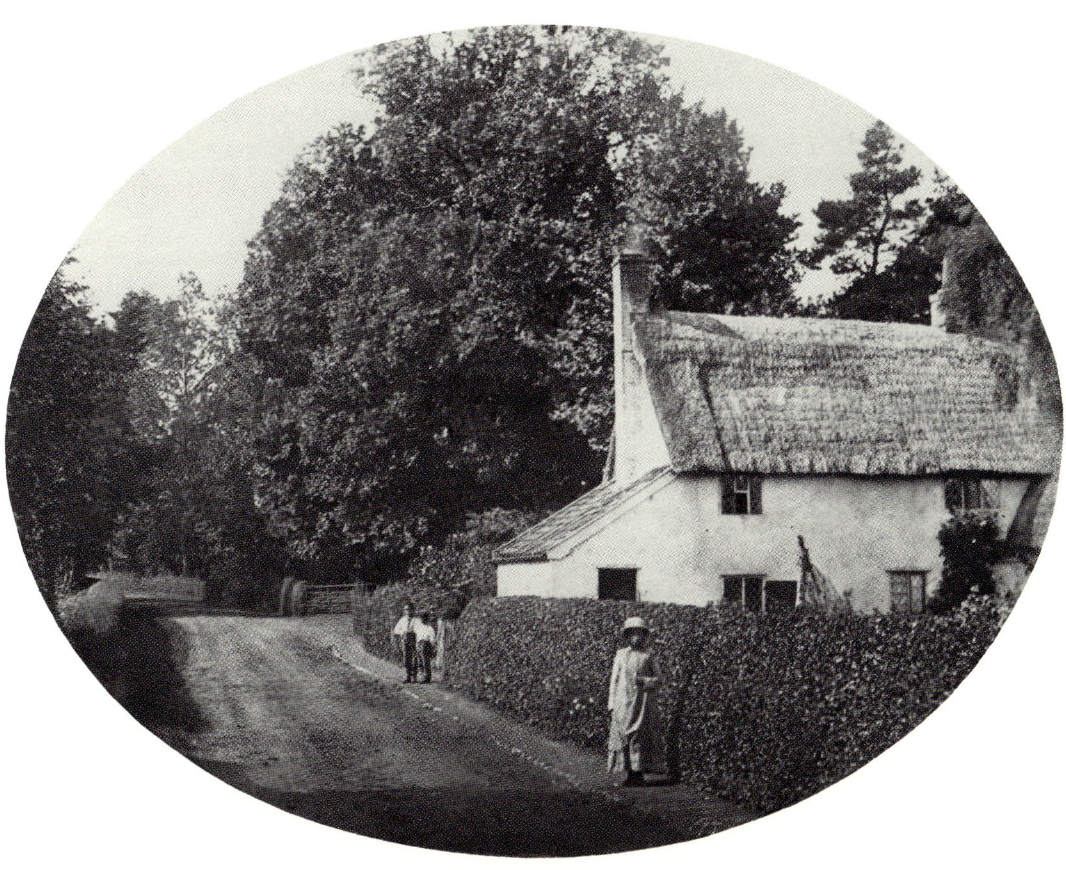

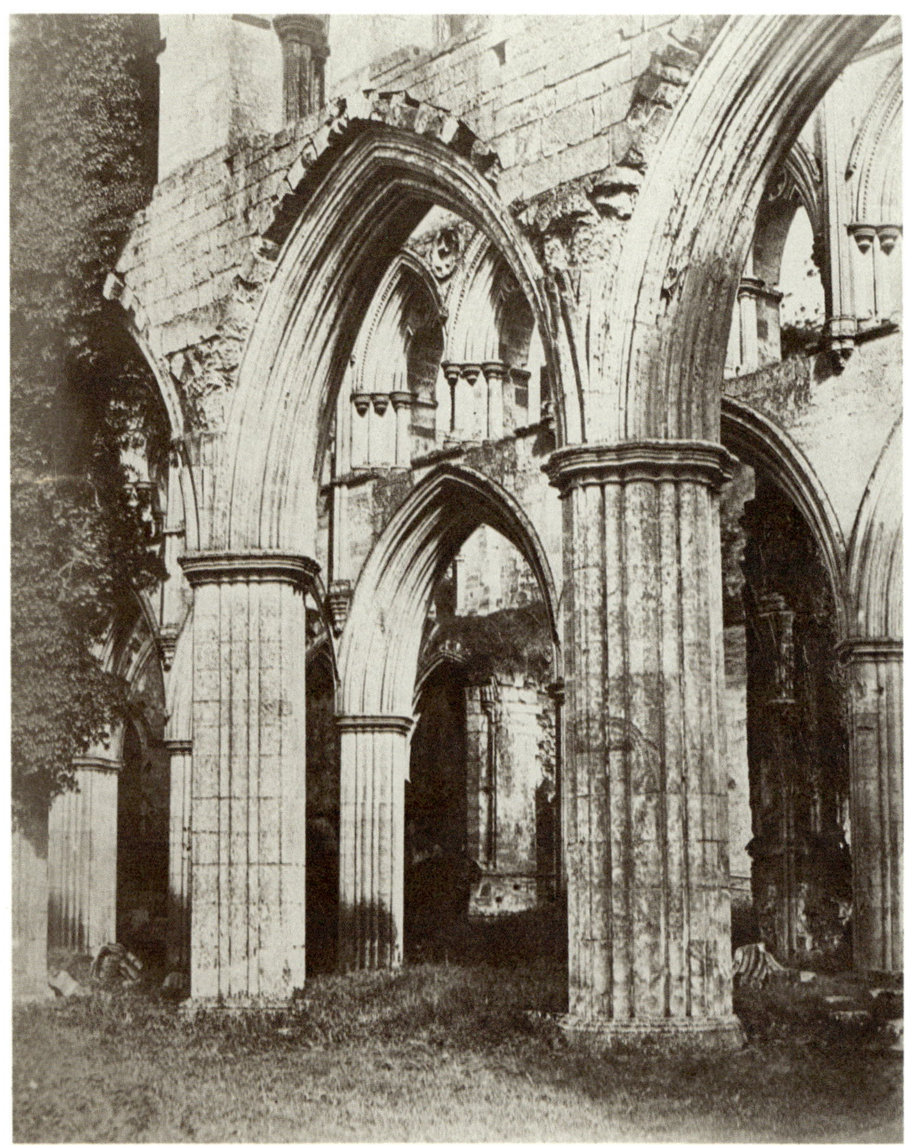

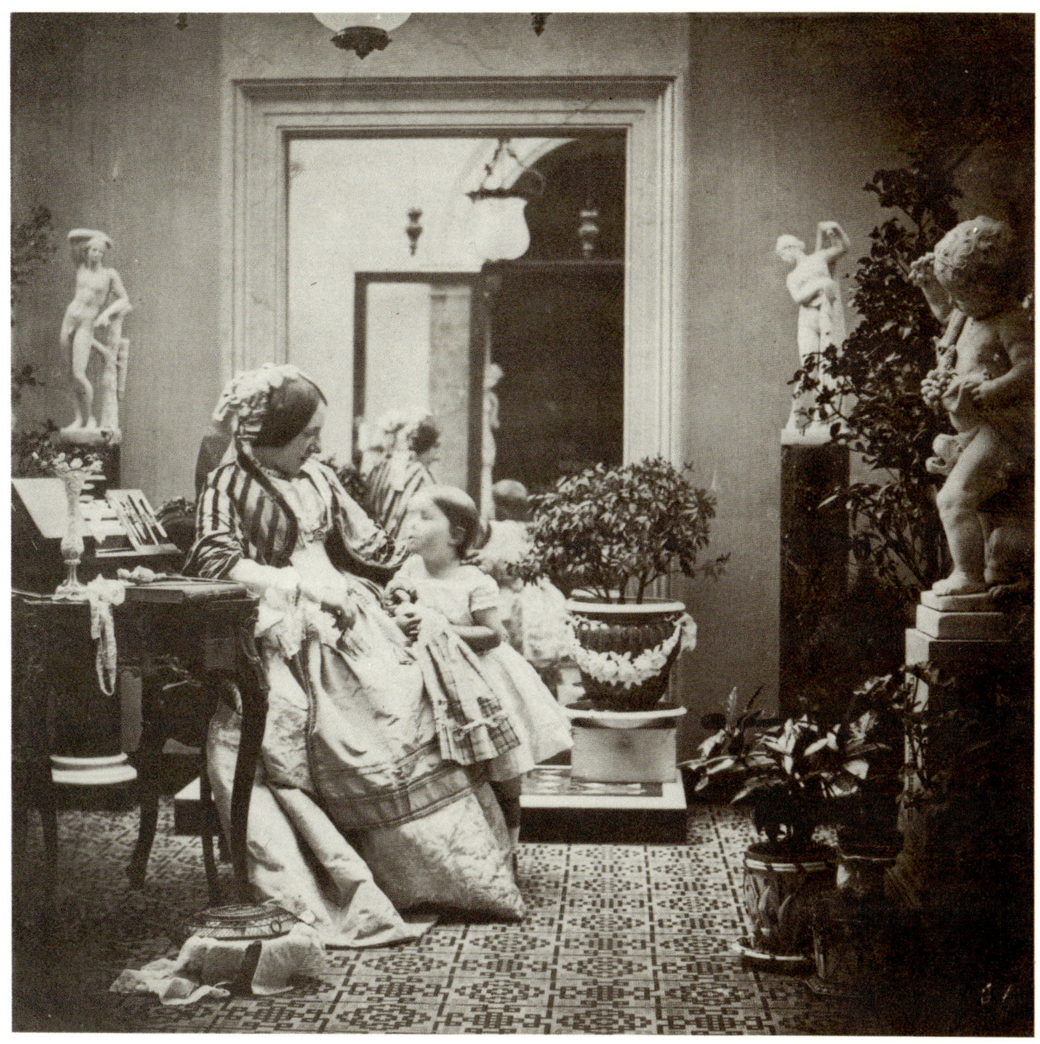

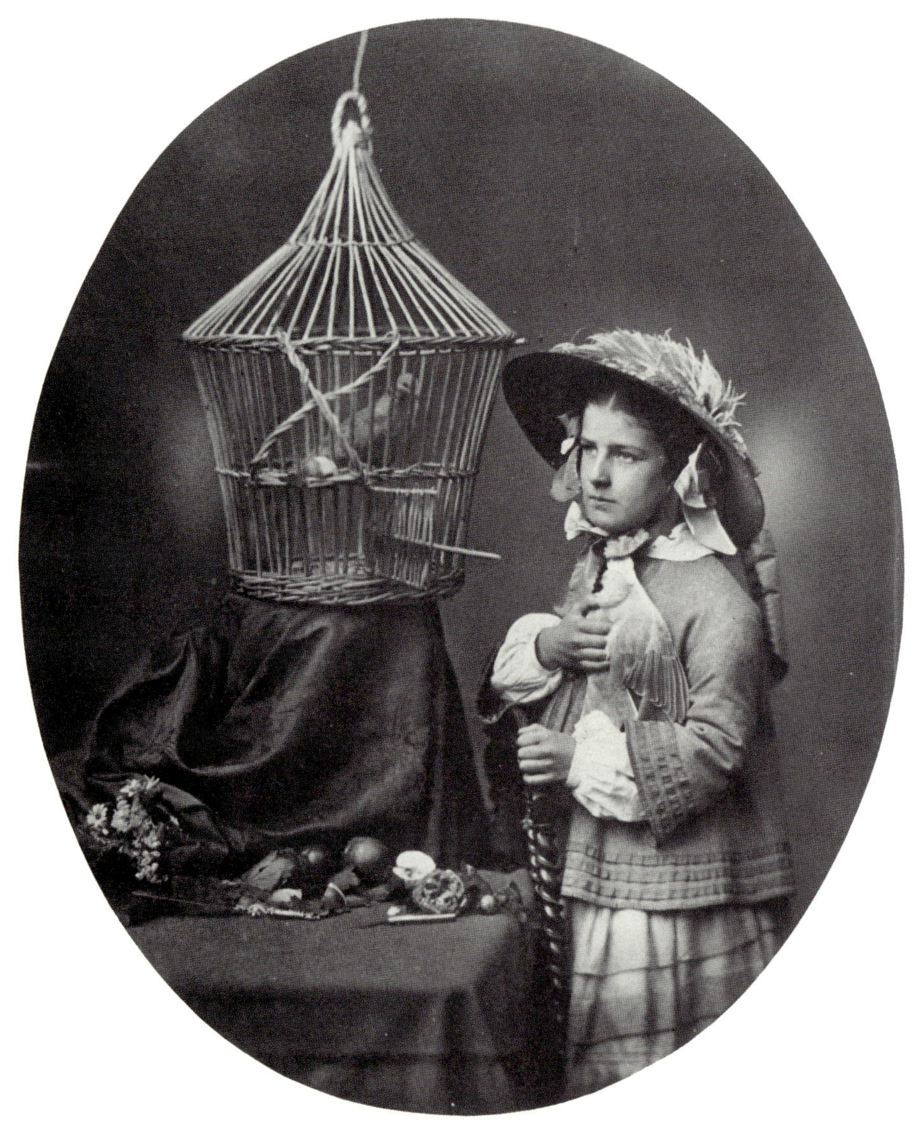

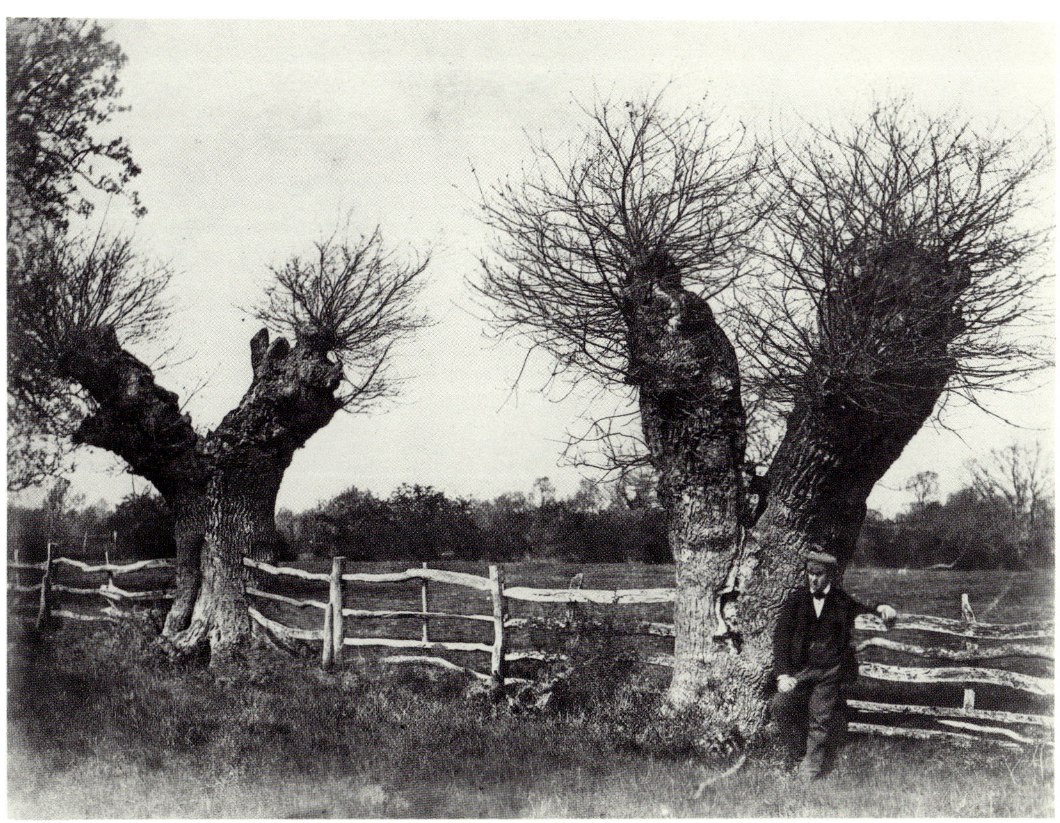

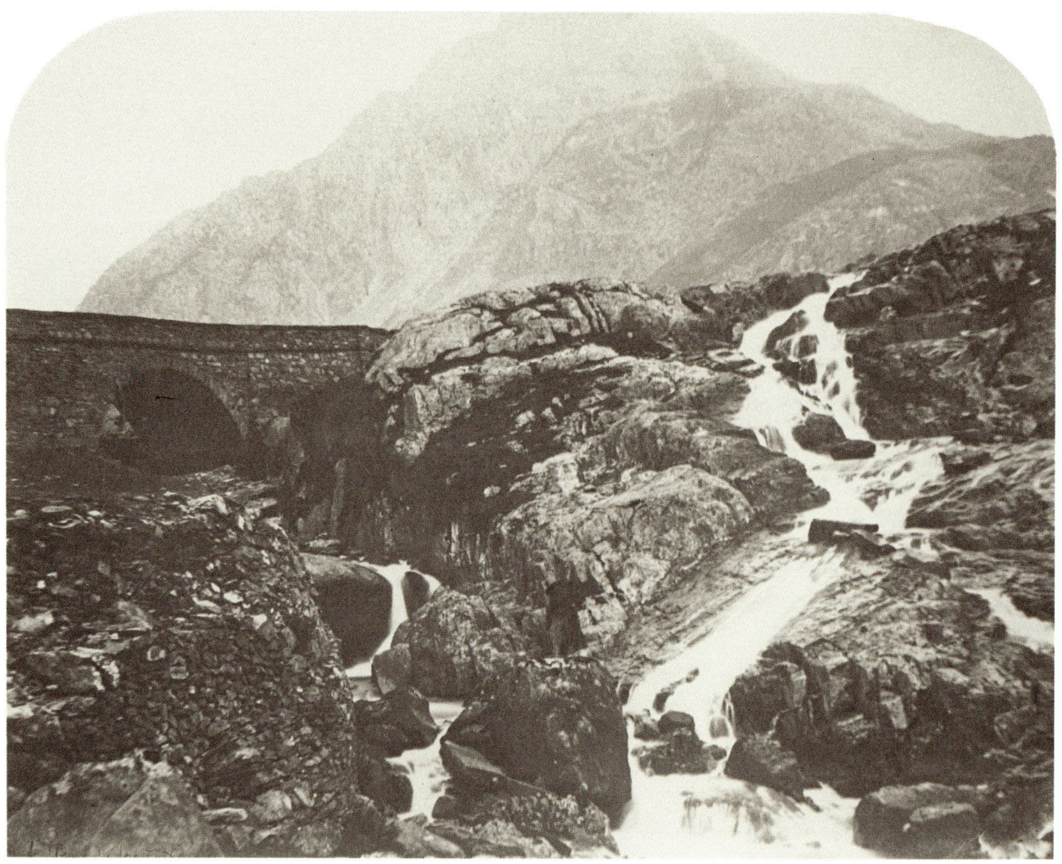

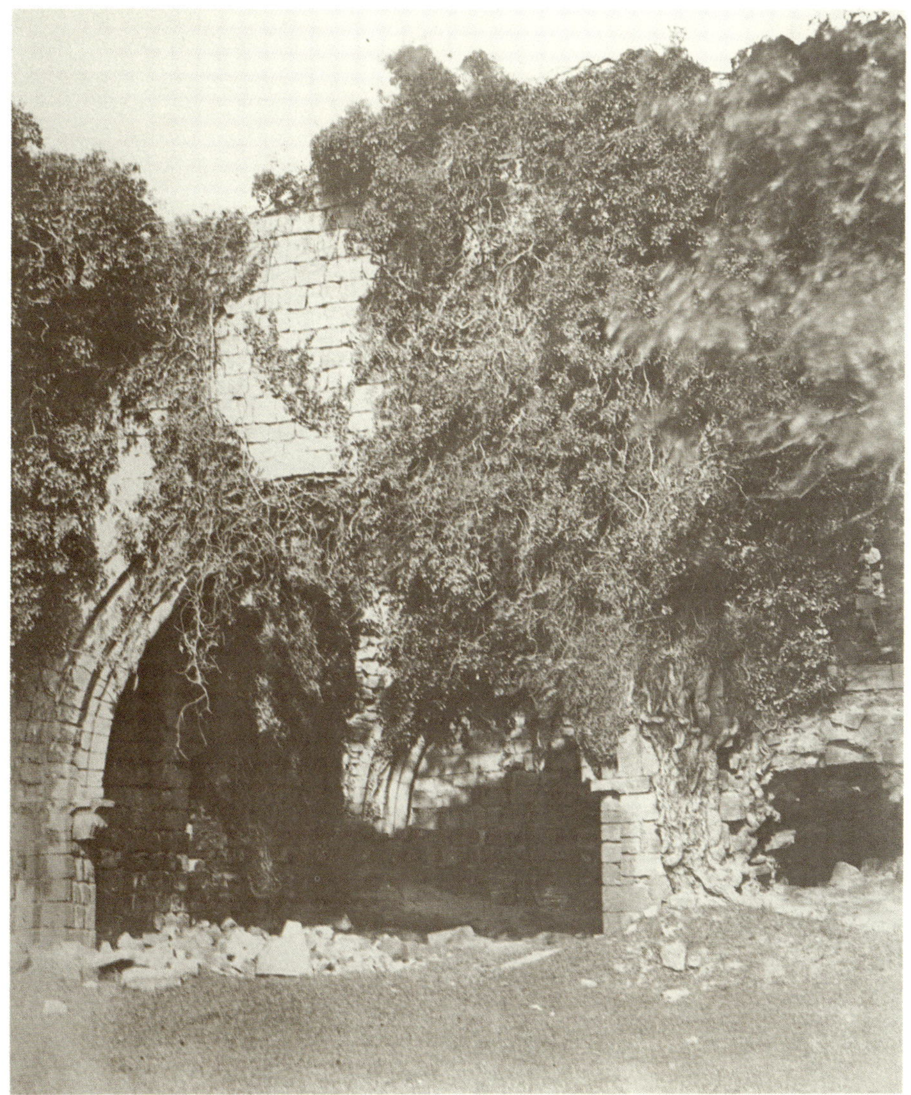

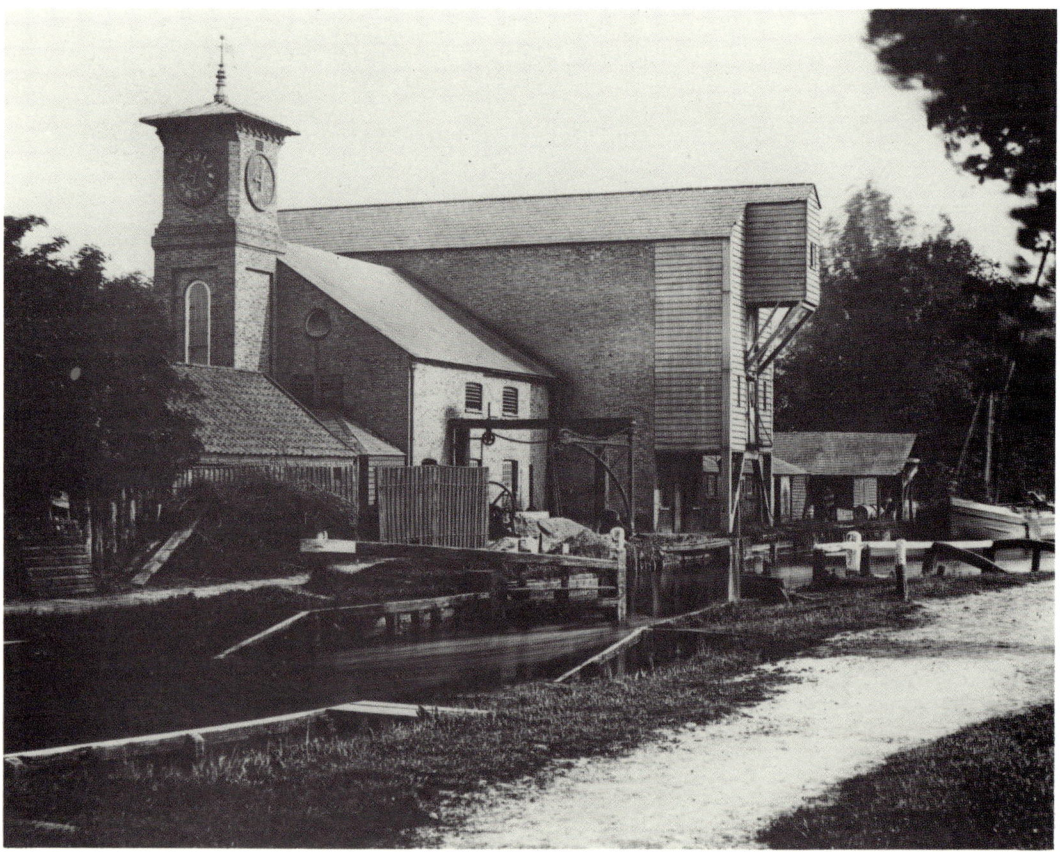

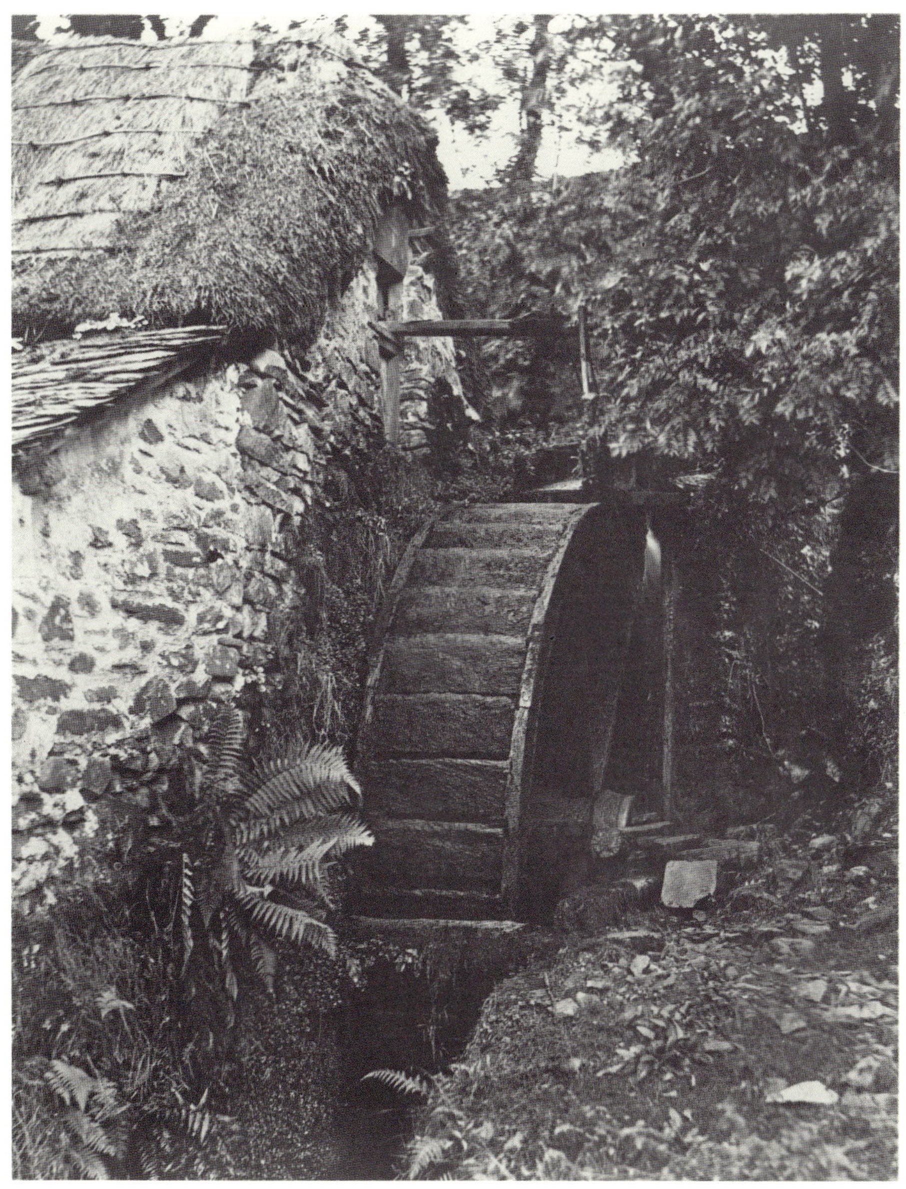

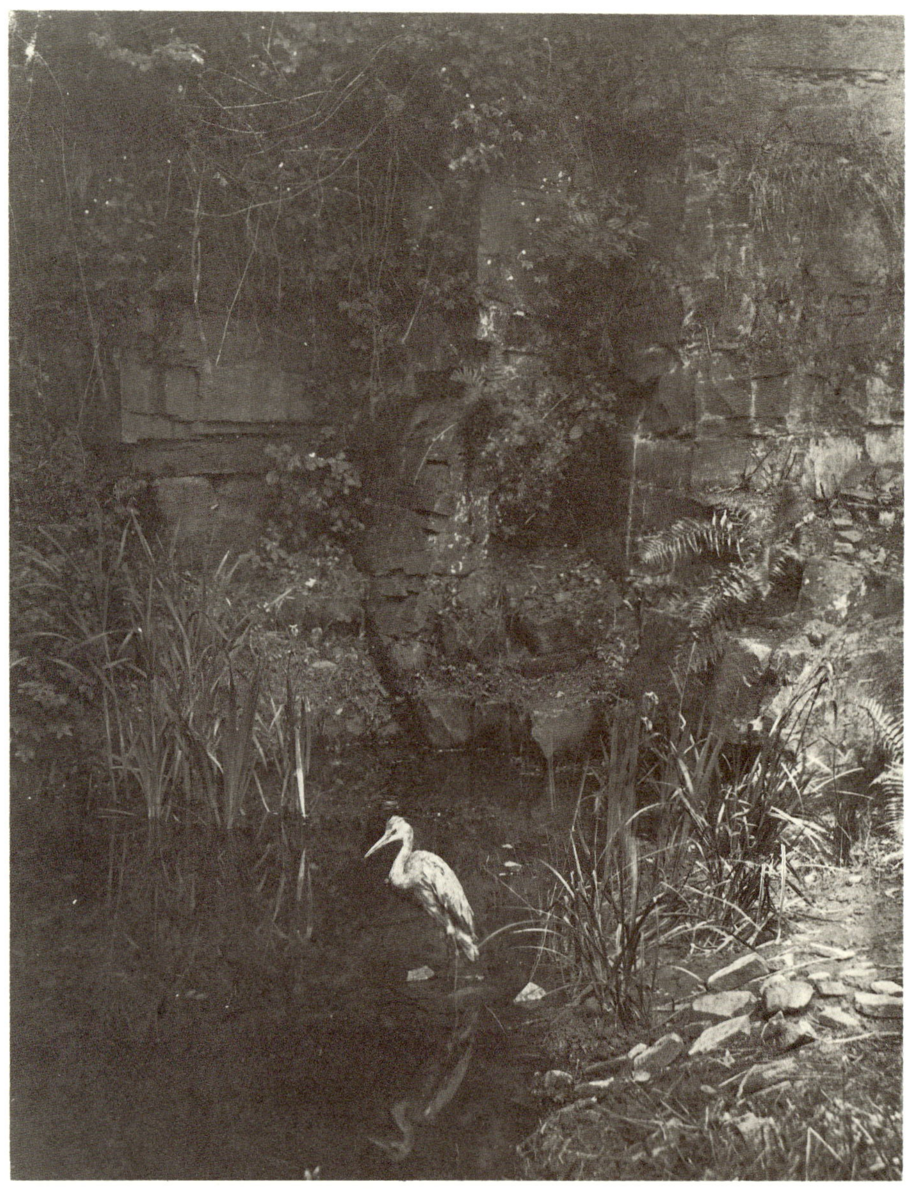

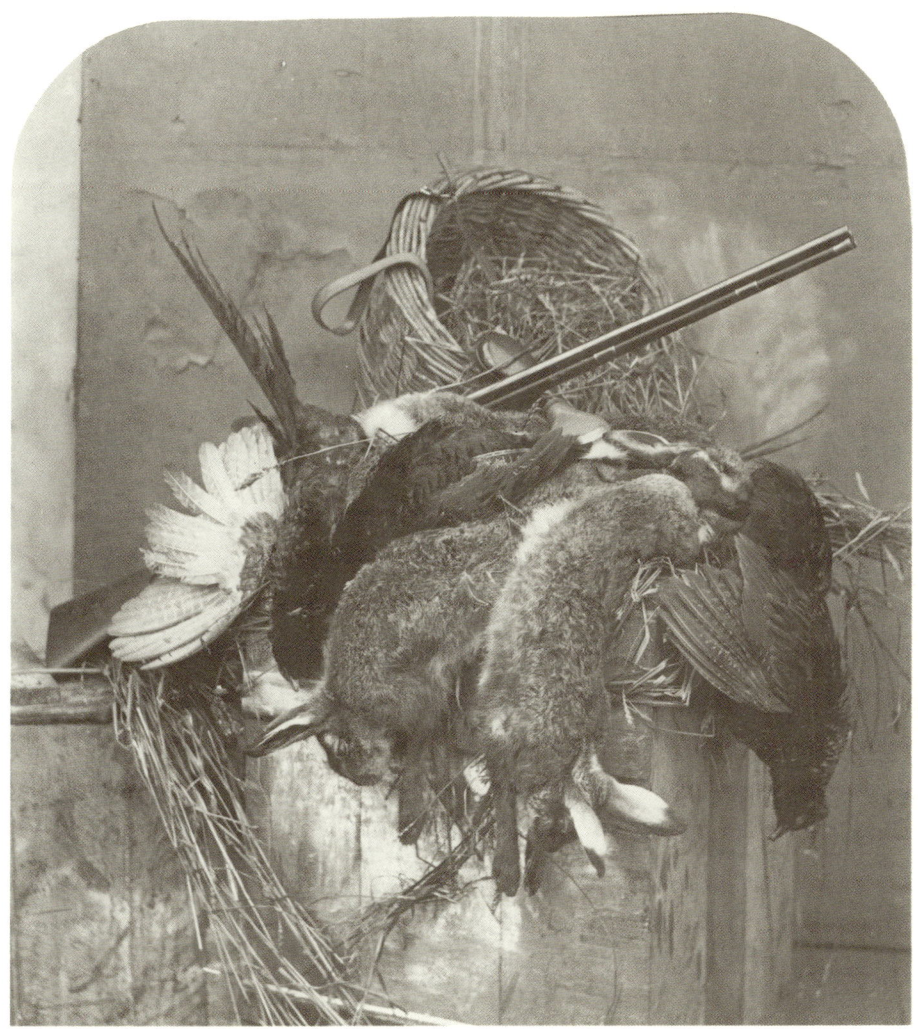

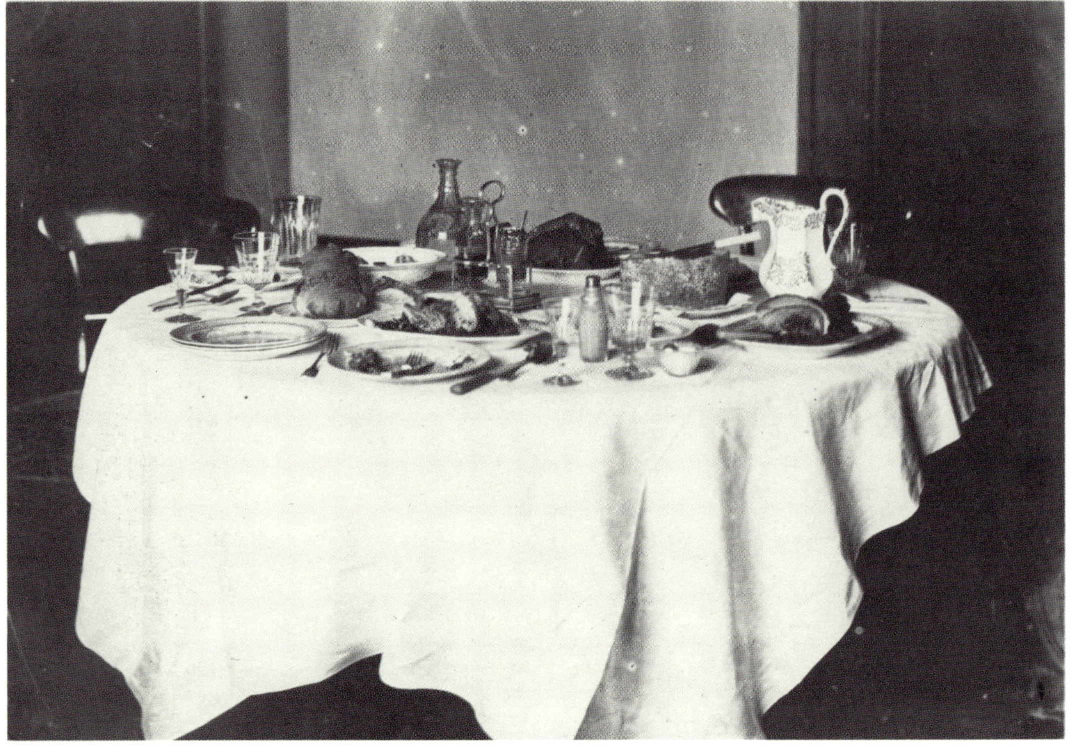

British amateurs in the 1850s prepared their own photographic materials. They worked with paper negatives using modifications of Fox Talbot's process, or with glass negatives using variations of Scott Archer's collodion process. Paper negatives were convenient, lightweight and durable; but the grain of the paper became part of the image. Prints from paper negatives could be quite detailed, but lacked the sharpness and clarity of those from glass negatives. Collodion provided a way to attach the photographic emulsion to a glass plate, but it was insolulable when dry; the plate had to be sensitized, exposed and developed within about twenty minutes. Collodion was faster than paper processes and was quickly adopted for portraits and figure studies. Cumbersome tent darkrooms allowed photographers to use this more precise process in the field, but some preferred paper or slower "dry" collodion negatives which could be developed at home. Contact prints were made by exposing sensitized paper, sandwiched in a frame with the negative, to the sun. The print was then fixed and was often toned. The amateurs used some version of the salted paper process in which the photo-sensitive materials are in the paper, or the albumen process in which an emulsion of egg white keeps the chemicals on top of the paper.

NEGATIVE PROCESSES

Paper negative: This term is used for prints which have some evidence of the grain of paper. Wax paper or waxed paper are not identified unless we have some evidence from annotations or contemporary sources that the photographers were using these processes. It is very difficult to judge from positives whether the paper was waxed, and it is not possible to tell from the negatives themselves whether they were waxed before or after exposure.

Collodion: The term collodion is used for all prints which appear to have been printed from glass negatives (identifiable by the absence of texture or, in some cases, by defects peculiar to collodion like dust spots, pouring marks, streaks or peeling emulsions). We are using collodion rather than the generic "glass negative" because there is no evidence that the photographers included here exhibited or exchanged prints made from albumen or other glass processes. So-called "dry" collodion (actually wet collodion with an agent added to retard drying) cannot be distinguished from wet collodion in a print or negative. When dry collodion processes like oxymel or syruped collodion are identified, it is because there is documentary evidence that the photographer used it for that particular negative.

PRINT PROCESSES

Salted Paper: All prints which have a matte surface and in which the image seems to be in, rather than on the surface of the paper, are identified as salted paper.

Albumen prints: Prints in which the image seems to be on top of the paper are identified as albumen prints. We have distinguished between lightly albumenized prints and albumen prints because many prints of the 1850s have almost no sheen. In photographic literature of the time, amateurs like George Shadbolt objected to the "vulgar glare" of albumen while recognizing its capacity for improved definition.

Toning: Gold toning enhances the stability of prints and gives them a deeper colour. The colour imparted by gold and other toning could vary from pale brown to browns of a deep purple, blue or even black cast depending upon factors including: the strength of the light at the time of printing; the sizing in the paper (English papers were usually sized with gelatine, which gave a warmer tone than starch-sized French papers) or sizing added by the photographer; and the chemicals used in processing the print and the conditions under which the print was kept. We have not attempted to identify these differences in print appearance. The *Photographic Album for the Year 1857* provides evidence for the variety of appearances which similar processes could produce.

Fading: The first losses in photographic prints occur in the highlights rather than in the shadows. An extended range of middle tones is characteristic of prints of the 1850s which may make some of the prints appear faded to modern eyes accustomed to strong value contrasts. However, many of the prints have suffered some loss. Certain glues affected early prints; while in other cases, air-carried pollutants have seeped in and have faded the edges of prints stored in albums and portfolios.

There were no standard processes for negatives or prints during the 1850s. By 1857 "printed in the ordinary manner" meant on albumen paper with gold toning, but prepared materials were becoming available only at the end of this period, and there was as yet no agreement on what a photograph should look like. Prints of the 1850s show a marvellous variety of colours and surfaces.

Measurements: All measurements are in centimetres; height preceding width

Francis Bedford began his career as an architect and lithographer and ended it as a professional photographer. During the 1850s, when he was beginning his work in photography, he worked on several books illustrated by chromolithographs which are classics of colour printing. In 1862 he accompanied the Prince of Wales on his tour of the Middle East as a photographer. In the 1860s and after, his career as maker and publisher of photographic views flourished.

ANONYMOUS PHOTOGRAPHS FROM KING'S COLLEGE, COLLECTED BY CHARLES WHEATSTONE

Wheatstone was the inventor of a stereoscope which allowed full-sized prints to be viewed stereoscopically with the aid of mirrors. The collection he assembled and gave to King's College includes prints by Fenton, Percy and other early amateurs; comments in journals make it clear that Llewelyn made stereos of this type and other photographs show stylistic resemblances to the works of members of the exchange clubs.

1. UNIDENTIFIED PHOTOGRAPHER
    Monkey
    c. early-mid 1850s
    Lightly albumenized print of paper negative
    16.2 × 20.0 cm
    King's College, London, Wheatstone collection

2. UNIDENTIFIED PHOTOGRAPHER
    Algae (photomicrograph)
    c. early-mid 1850s
    Salted paper print of collodion negative
    19.5 × 15.6 cm (oval)
    King's College, London, Wheatstone collecton

3. UNIDENTIFIED PHOTOGRAPHER
    Algae (photomicrograph)
    c. early-mid 1850s
    Salted paper print of collodion negative
    19.7 × 15.5 cm (oval)
    King's College, London, Wheatstone collecton

4. UNIDENTIFIED PHOTOGRAPHER
    Raglan Castle
    c. early-mid 1850s
    Albumen print of collodion negative
    16.6 × 21.2 cm
    King's College, London, Wheatstone collection

MARK ANTHONY 1817-1886

Mark Anthony was an artist who exhibited works regularly at the Royal Academy.

5. MARK ANTHONY
    Wild Flowers
    From: *Photographic Album for the Year 1857*, no.3
    1856
    Albumen print of collodion negative ("Taken on collodion June 1856, weather sunny morning, exposure 25 seconds, developed with pyrogallic acid, lens French, focal length 15″, diameter combination 4½″ and diaphragm 1″, printed on Toogood's plain paper, Ammonio-Nitrate of Silver and Sel d'Or toning bath by Spencer.")
    20.8 × 15.7 cm
    International Museum of Photography at George Eastman House, Rochester, New York

6. FRANCIS BEDFORD
    Rievaulx Abbey
    Photographic Exchange Club print, 1857 exchange
    c. 1857
    Albumen print of collodion negative
    19.8 × 16.1 cm
    Art Institute of Chicago

7. FRANCIS BEDFORD
    Study of Plants
    Photographic Exchange Club print, 1858 exchange
    c. mid 1850s
    Albumen print of collodion negative
    16.4 × 22.0 cm
    Royal Photographic Society, Bath

8. FRANCIS BEDFORD
    At Pont y Pair, Bettws-y-Coed, North Wales
    From *Photographic Album for the Year 1857*, no.5
    1856
    Albumen print of collodion negative ("Taken on collodion (wet) in the middle of June 1856; weather bright sunny day, very hot, exposure one minute, development one grain solution pyrogallic acid, lens by Ross, focal length 15″, diameter 3″, diaphragm ⅜″. Printed on albumenized paper, coloured with gold.")
    19.4 × 23.8 cm
    International Museum of Photography at George Eastman House, Rochester, New York

9. FRANCIS BEDFORD
    Canterbury, Norman Staircase
    c. 1857
    Albumen print of collodion negative
    18.4 × 24.1 cm
    Stephen White, Los Angeles

10. FRANCIS BEDFORD
    Cottages at Aberglaslyn
    c. late 1850s
    From: Philip H. Delamotte (ed), *The Sunbeam: A Book of Photographs from Nature*, London, Chapman & Hall, 1859, pl. 7
    Albumen print of collodion negative
    19.1 × 23.9 cm
    Royal Photographic Society, Bath

11. FRANCIS BEDFORD
    Chagford, Holy S. Mill
    c. 1860s
    Albumen print of collodion negative
    16.2 × 21.6 cm
    Metropolitan Museum of Art, New York

12. FRANCIS BEDFORD
    Stratford on Avon Church from the Avon
    c. 1860s
    Albumen print of collodion negative

18.8 × 28.0 cm
International Museum of Photography at George Eastman
House, Rochester, New York
13. FRANCIS BEDFORD
(view of Torquay, newspaper clipping and wood engraving)
From: *Pictorial Illustrations of Torquay and its
Neighbourhood*
c. 1870s
Albumen print of collodion negative
10.0 × 14.4 cm
International Museum of Photography at George Eastman
House, Rochester, New York
14. FRANCIS BEDFORD
(Frontispiece)
From: Joshua Fawcett, *The Churches of York by
W. Monkhouse and F. Bedford with historical and
architectural notes.* York, H. Smith, 1843
c. 1843
Lithograph
26.1 × 19.4 cm
Victoria and Albert Museum, London
15. FRANCIS BEDFORD and P. H. DELAMOTTE
Objects in Silver by Fromont Meurice of Paris
From: Mathew Digby Wyatt, *Industrial Arts of the XIX
Century at the Great Exhibition*, London, Day and Son,
1851-3, pl. 137
Chromolithograph (lithograph by Bedford after drawing by
Delamotte)
40.7 × 26.6 cm
Victoria and Albert Museum, London
16. FRANCIS BEDFORD
The Bridge at Llanrwst
c. late 1850s, 1860s
Albumen prints of collodion negatives
Stereo: each image 7.3 × 7.1 cm
Russell Norton, New Haven
17. FRANCIS BEDFORD
Beddgelert, the Rustic Bridge and Mountains
c. late 1850s, 1860s
Albumen prints of collodion negatives
Stereo: each image 7.9 × 7.9 cm
International Museum of Photography at George Eastman
House, Rochester, New York
18. FRANCIS BEDFORD
Bettwys-y-Coed, Falls on the Llugwy
c. late 1850s, 1860s
Albumen prints of collodion negatives
Stereo: each image 8 × 8 cm
International Museum of Photography at George Eastman
House, Rochester, New York
19. FRANCIS BEDFORD
Ilfracombe, the Harbour from the Pier
c. late 1850s, 1860s
Albumen prints of collodion negatives
Stereo: each image 8.2 × 7.9 cm
Russell Norton, New Haven
20. FRANCIS BEDFORD
Conway, the Castle from the Quay
c. late 1850s, 1860s
Albumen prints of collodion negatives
Stereo: each image 7.9 × 7.9 cm

Russell Norton, New Haven
21. FRANCIS BEDFORD
Welsh Group: Market Women
c. late 1850s, 1860s
Albumen prints of collodion negatives
Stereos: each image 7.4 × 7.4 cm
Russell Norton, New Haven

W. G. CAMPBELL active 1850s

Campbell was a London member of the Photographic Society.
He also belonged to the Photographic Exchange Club and
contributed to the exchange within the Photographic Society,
the Photographic Club. All of the four pictures he contributed to
the Exchange Club are picturesque views, while he sent a genre
scene to the *Photographic Album for the Year 1857*.
22. W. G. CAMPBELL
The Lesson
From: *Photographic Album for the Year 1857*, no. 6
1856
Albumen print of collodion negative ("Collodion, May 1856,
11 AM, weather cloudy, exposure 7 seconds, developed by
pyrogallic acid, lens by Ross, focal length 13", diameter 3¼",
diaphragm 2½". Printed on Marion's Paper sensitized with a
60 grain solution of nitrate of silver and chloride of gold by
W.G.C.")
Oval 15.1 × 17.7 cm
International Museum of Photography at George Eastman
House, Rochester, New York
23. W. G. CAMPBELL
Sandwich, Kent
Photographic Exchange Club print, 1858 exchange
c. mid 1850s
Lightly albumenized print of paper negative
19.5 × 24.6 cm
Royal Photographic Society, Bath

JOSEPH CUNDALL 1818-1875

Cundall was a publisher who produced many illustrated
books, including some illustrated by photographs. He founded
the Photographic Institution, an organization for the teaching
and display of photography, which offered his own services along
with those of Delamotte and later Howlett and Downes in
undertaking photographic commisions.
24. JOSEPH CUNDALL
An Evening Tale
1855
Albumen print of collodion negative
23.4 × 18.2 cm
International Museum of Photography at George Eastman
House, Rochester, New York
Note: annotated on mount: J. Cundall phot. August 1855
25. JOSEPH CUNDALL
Highlanders
From: *The Photographic Album for the Year 1857*, no. 9
1856
Albumen print of collodion negative ("Collodion, June 1856,
weather fine, exposed 10 seconds, developed with pyrogallic
acid, lens by Ross, focal length 15", diameter 4½", diaphragm
1", printed by the ordinary method and toned with Gold.")

24.0 × 19.8 cm
International Museum of Photography at George Eastman
House, Rochester, New York
26. JOSEPH CUNDALL
Bilbury Bridge
Albumen print of collodion negative
From: Joseph Cundall, *Twenty Views in Gloucestershire*,
London, Cundall, 1854
1854
Round: diameter 16 cm
Harrison Horblit, Ridgefield Connecticut
Note: The preface states: "These Photographic Views were
taken at the request of an eminent Engineer, to be laid, in
Evidence, before a Committee of the House of Commons.
They were produced by the collodion process in the third
week of March, and were all developed in a Post-chaise."

FRANCIS EDMOND CURREY 1814-1896

Currey was the Duke of Devonshire's agent for his Irish
properties. He lived at Lismore Castle in County Waterford,
Ireland. Undoubtedly his still life photographs of game, as well
as his views of the castle and its surroundings, reflect the
activities of the place. After the demise of the Photographic
Exchange Club, Currey became a member of the larger and
more impersonal Amateur Photographic Association.
27. F. E. CURREY
Still Life of a Bird
Amateur Photographic Association print 313/14
c. 1860
Albumen print of collodion negative
20.3 × 14.7 cm
International Museum of Photography at George Eastman
House, Rochester, New York
28. F. E. CURREY
Lismore Castle and surroundings (from an album)
c. mid 1850s
Four albumen prints of collodion negatives
20.8 × 17.1 cm
Sean Sexton, United Kingdom

PHILIP HENRY DELAMOTTE 1821-1889

The son of an artist, Delamotte began and ended his career as
an artist, teacher and author of books on subjects like sketching
for amateurs. During the 1850s he was active as a photographer
while he was making drawings for illustrated publications like
Wyatt's *Industrial Arts of the XIX Century* (no. 15). After he
accepted a post as Professor of Drawing at King's College in
1855, he gave up his affiliation with the Photographic Institution,
but continued to produce photographic publications like *Views in
Oxford*, 1857, and *The Sunbeam*, a periodical, 1858 and 1859.
29. PHILIP H. DELAMOTTE
Innocence
From: *Photographic Album for the Year 1855*, no. 27
1855
Albumen print of collodion negative
Oval 18.7 × 15.7 cm
Royal Photographic Society, Bath
30. PHILIP H. DELAMOTTE
Evening

c. mid 1850s
Albumen print of collodion negative
21.2 × 14.7 cm
Metropolitan Museum of Art, New York
Note: This photograph was taken at Llewelyn's estate,
Penllergare, in South Wales.
31. PHILIP H. DELAMOTTE
Burnham Beeches
c. 1852
Albumen print of collodion negative
19.6 × 23.1 cm
Metropolitan Museum of Art, New York
Note: Annotated on mount: "Collodion, Burnham Beeches,
P. H. Delamotte, July 1852."
32. PHILIP H. DELAMOTTE
Brinckburn Priory
c. mid 1850s
Albumen print of collodion negative
20.7 × 25.1 cm
Metropolitan Museum of Art, New York
Note: Annotated on mount: "Collodion, Delamotte,
Brinckburn Priory."
33. PHILIP H. DELAMOTTE
Croxton Abbey
early 1850s
Albumen print of collodion negative
20.6 × 15.2 cm
Metropolitan Museum of Art, New York
Note: Annotated on mount: "Croxton Abbey, 'Only to him
seated under this silent arcade is all around a poem, he
symbolizes the nation; he rests upon those time-stained
stones as the future rests upon the past. Behind him in the
depths of the arch all is shadows and ruin, before him all is
sunshine and life.' From La Lumière"
34. PHILIP H. DELAMOTTE
Workmen in the Grounds
From: Philip H. Delamotte, *Photographic Reports of the
Progress of the Crystal Palace Sydenham*, London, The
Photographic Institution, 1855, no. 7
c. 1852
Salted paper print of collodion negative
15.4 × 20.5 cm
Greater London Council History Library, London
35. PHILIP H. DELAMOTTE
The Bear
From: *Photographic Reports*, no. 107
c. 1853-5
Albumen print of collodion negative
28.7 × 14.1 cm
Greater London Council History Library, London
36. PHILIP H. DELAMOTTE
Arrival of Plants – the Cyclas Revolta
From: *Photographic Reports*, no. 118
c. 1853-5
Albumen print of collodion negative
19.8 × 24.1 cm
Greater London Council History Library, London
37. PHILIP H. DELAMOTTE
Head of one of the Colossi of Monte Cavallo Rome, by
Phidias
From: *Photographic Reports*, no. 102

Lightly albumenized print of collodion negative
c. 1853-5
15.7 × 20.5 cm
Greater London Council History Library, London

38. PHILIP H. DELAMOTTE
The Upper Gallery
From: *Photographic Reports*, no. 35
c. 1853-5
Lightly albumenized print of collodion negative
27.0 × 23.4 cm
Greater London Council History Library, London

39. PHILIP H. DELAMOTTE
Titian, Design for a Picture
From: Henry Reveley, *The Reveley Collection of Drawings,
at Brangwyn North Wales*, photographed by Philip H.
Delamotte and T. Frederick Hardwich, London, Bell and
Daldy, 1858.
1858
Salted paper print of collodion negative
22.7 × 17.2 cm
Victoria and Albert Museum, London

40. PHILIP H. DELAMOTTE AND JOSEPH CUNDALL
Kirkstall Abbey. Ruins on the South Side
From: Philip H. Delamotte and Joseph Cundall,
A Photographic Tour among the Abbeys of Yorkshire (with
Descriptive Notices by John Richard Walbran, FSA),
London, Bell and Dalday, 1856, pl. 16
c. 1856
Albumen print of collodion negative
29.7 × 23.4 cm
National Gallery of Canada, Ottawa

41. PHILIP H. DELAMOTTE AND JOSEPH CUNDALL
Rievaulx Abbey, looking across the Choir
From: Philip H. Delamotte and Joseph Cundall,
A Photographic Tour, pl. 20
c. 1856
Albumen print of collodion negative
27.3 × 22.9 cm
National Gallery of Canada, Ottawa

HUGH WELCH DIAMOND 1809-1886

Dr. Diamond was an important early publicist of photography.
His instructions for the calotype and collodion processes,
published in *Notes and Queries*, provided a starting point for
many photographers. He was host to regular informal
gatherings of photographers. As head of the Surrey County
Lunatic Asylum, he used photography to record and treat
patients. He was also an antiquary and was interested in the use
of phtotography to record monuments and objects. Between
1858 and 1869 he edited the *Journal of the Photographic Society*
which became the *Photographic Journal*.

42. HUGH W. DIAMOND
The Cromlech at Plas Newydd, Anglesea
1854
Salted paper print of paper negative
13.5 × 15.9 cm
Society of Antiquaries, London

43. HUGH W. DIAMOND
Shakespeare's House

Photographic Exchange Club print, 1857 exchange
1854
Albumen print of paper negative
25.0 × 19.8 cm
Royal Photographic Society, Bath
Note: an alternative view was presented by Dr. Diamond to
the Society of Antiquaries in 1854, cf. *Proceedings* III, p. 71

44. HUGH W. DIAMOND
Cavalier's Glove
c. 1854
Albumen print of paper negative
9.4 × 17.7 cm
Society of Antiquaries, London
Note: Presented to the Society of Antiquaries in January
1854. Annotated on mount: "One of a pair discovered in a
house in Fore Street, Wellington, Somerset in 1820."

45. HUGH W. DIAMOND
Early English Comb carved in Ivory
c. 1854
Albumen print of paper negative
12.2 × 16.0 cm
Society of Antiquaries, London
Note: "Dr. Diamond presented to the Society a photograph
of the Mediaeval comb recently exhibited by Mr. Broocke,
his first contribution as Honorary Photographer to the
Society," *Proceedings*, III, pp. 54, 57.

46. HUGH W. DIAMOND
Copy of a Bust of Her Majesty Queen Victoria by Joseph
Durham Esq. F.S.A.
Photographic Exchange Club print, 1858 exchange
1857
Albumen print of collodion negative
20.2 × 14.5 cm
Norfolk Record Office, Norwich
Note: The photograph was also frontispiece to the
Photographic Album for the Year 1857. "Taken on collodion
June 1857, weather fine. Exposure five minutes, developed
in pyrogallic acid. Lens by Ross, focal length 12″, diameter
2½″, diaphragm ⅝″, printed in the ordinary way by Dr.
Diamond".

47. HUGH W. DIAMOND
Copy of a print by Dürer 1511
c. mid 1850s
Albumen print of collodion negative
15.1 × 10.9 cm
Norfolk Records Office, Norwich, Eaton collection

48. HUGH W. DIAMOND
Page of portraits of the insane
From: album, Royal Medical and Chiurgical Society
Photographs A.
Medical, etc.
Albumen prints of collodion negatives
67.6 × 52.7 cm
Royal College of Medicine, London

THOMAS DAMANT EATON 1800-1871

Eaton retired from business in 1846 and devoted himself to his
amateur pursuits. Although he was most active in musical
societies, he had literary and scientific interests and painted and
photographed. He was president of the Norwich Photographic

Society. His pictures show his native Norwich where he was a
well known figure.
49. T. D. EATON
     Camera Sktches (negative and title page)
     1845
     Paper (calotype) negative
     7.5 × 7.7 cm
     Norwich Central Library, Local History Library
50. T. D. EATON
     Thorwaldsen's Venus
     c. early 1850s
     Salted paper print of paper negative
     17.0 × 10.1 cm
     Norwich Central Library, Local History Library
51. T. D. EATON
     The Erpingham Gate
     Photographic Exchange Club print, 1855 exchange
     c. 1855
     Lightly albumenized print of paper negative
     21.0 × 16.3 cm
     Norwich Central Library, Local History Library

ROGER FENTON 1819-1869

   Fenton's career bridges amateur and professional photography
in the 1850s. He was instrumental in founding the Photographic
Society and participated in exchanges within it. The wide range
of his work covers all the standard amateur subjects. He also
photographed the Crimean War, objects in the British Museum
and the royal family on commission. He produced stereos and
views for sale and contributed prints to the *Photographic
Album, Photographic Art Treasures* and other publications.
Fenton's eclectic approach did not bring him great commercial
success, but it is not clear whether disillusionment with
photography or some other reason motivated his announcement
in 1862 that he was giving up photography to return to the
practice of law.
52. ROGER FENTON
     Birth of Saint John ("Copied from a carving on yellow hone
     stone by Albert Dürer in the British Museum. The
     photograph is the same size as the original.")
     From: *Photographic Album for the Year 1857*, no. 14
     1857
     Albumen print of collodion negative ("Collodion, May 1857,
     exposure 2½ minutes, developed by pyrogallic acid. Lens
     by Ross, focal length 20″, diameter 4″, diaphragm ¾″. Printed
     on albumenized paper with chloride and nitrate of silver by
     R. Fenton.")
     19.3 × 13.6 cm
     International Museum of Photography at George Eastman
     House, Rochester, New York
53. ROGER FENTON
     Hush Lightly Tread
     From: *Photographic Art Treasures*, 1857
     c. 1856
     Photogalvanographic engraving
     19.1 × 16.0 cm (plate)
     International Museum of Photography at George Eastman
     House, Rochester, New York
54. ROGER FENTON
     Still Life of Game

c. mid 1850s
Albumen print of collodion negative
36.3 × 32.8 cm
Royal Photographic Society, Bath
55. ROGER FENTON
     A Memento of Furness
     c. mid 1850s
     Albumen print of collodion negative
     28.0 × 28.0 cm
     Royal Photographic Society, Bath
56. ROGER FENTON
     (Waterfall in a wood)
     c. mid 1850s
     Albumen print of collodion negative
     28.5 × 28.1 cm
     Royal Photographic Society, Bath
57. ROGER FENTON [attributed to]
     Dead Stag
     c. 1852
     Lightly albumenized print of collodion negative
     16.2 × 21.5 cm
     King's College, London
58. ROGER FENTON [attributed to]
     Dead Stag
     c. 1852
     Albumen print of collodion negative
     16.2 × 21.2 cm
     King's College, London
     Note: Fenton exhibited: Dead Stag, Zoological Gdns. in the
     Exhibition of Recent Specimens of Photography 1852 (no.
     211). He also took many pictures of deer shot by Prince
     Albert.
59. ROGER FENTON
     Furness Abbey
     From: William and Mary Howitt, *Ruined Abbeys and
     Castles of Great Britain*: The photographic illustrations by
     Bedford, Sedgefield, Wilson, Fenton and others, London,
     A. W. Bennett, 1862, p. 217
     c. late 1850s
     Albumen print of collodion negative
     Oval 7.0 × 8.5 cm
     International Museum of Photography at George Eastman
     House, Rochester, New York

JOSEPH JAMES FORRESTER
(Baron de Forrester in Portugal) 1809-1862

   Forrester was a wine merchant whose trade in port wine
required him to spend much time in Portugal. He surveyed the
river Douro with the aim of improving its navigability. His
documentation through maps and lithographs was followed in
the 1850s by photographs — not only of the river, but also of
objects of antiquarian interest.
60. J. J. FORRESTER
     Margins of the Douro, near to the Cachao de Valeira
     From: *Photographic Album for the Year 1855*, no. 33
     1855
     Albumen print of paper negative ("Calotype 14 August
     1855, 20 minutes past 2 o'clock, sunshiny, exposure 6
     minutes. Developed by Dr. Diamond's process. Lens by
     Ross, focal length 12″, diameter 2½″,

diaphragm ⅝″)
16.3 × 21.2 cm
Royal Photographic Society, Bath
Note: The accompanying text reads: "This photograph is
one of 220 views originally intended to illustrate the
author's survey of the Douro, and to exhibit the bed and
margins of that river in all seasons."

61. J. J. FORRESTER
On the Douro
Photographic Exchange Club print, 1855-6 exchange
c. 1855
Salted paper print of paper negative
12.7 × 17.5 cm
Norfolk Record Office, Norwich, Eaton collection

62. J. J. FORRESTER
Serra Convent, Oporto before the Siege
From: Joseph James Forrester, *Portuguese Scenery with
Illustrative Notes*, Oporto, by the Author; London,
J. Dickinson, 1835
1835
Lithograph
14.2 × 19.0 cm
National Art Library, Victoria and Albert Museum, London

ROBERT HOWLETT 1831-1858

When Howlett died at the age of twenty-seven, his death
certificate listed his occupation as "photographic artist".
The variety of his productions is evidence of the lack of fixed
definitions for this profession in the 1850s. He and the
publisher, Cundall, issued pictures under the name Cundall
and Howlett. Howlett documented the progress of the
steamship the *Great Eastern*, took portraits and costume
pictures and was admired for his reproductions of works of
art. He published a book on methods of printing pictures.
He also belonged to exchange clubs and made picturesque
landscapes like those of the amateurs.

63. ROBERT HOWLETT
Barn at the Bee Hive, Mickleham
c. mid 1850s
Albumen print of collodion negative
18.2 × 23.6 cm
International Museum of Photography at George Eastman
House, Rochester, New York

64. ROBERT HOWLETT
Farm Yard at the Bee Hive, Mickleham
c. 1850s
Lightly albumenized print of collodion negative
18.8 × 24.3 cm
International Museum of Photography at George Eastman
House, Rochester, New York

65. ROBERT HOWLETT
Valley of the Mole
1855
Albumen print of collodion negative
20.4 × 17.0 cm
International Museum of Photography at George Eastman
House, Rochester, New York
Note: This view is a variant of one which Howlett
contributed to the
Photographic Album for the Year 1855.

66. ROBERT HOWLETT
Dover
Photographic Exchange Club print, 1858 exchange
c. mid 1850s
Albumen print of collodion negative
20.7 × 26.2 cm
Royal Photographic Society, Bath

67. ROBERT HOWLETT
The *Great Eastern* under construction
c. 1857
Albumen print of collodion negative
21.6 × 26.4 cm
International Museum of Photography at George Eastman
House, Rochester, New York

68. ROBERT HOWLETT
Isambard Kingdom Brunel
c. 1857
Albumen print of collodion negative
Arched top: 28.6 × 22.9 cm
International Museum of Photography at George Eastman
House, Rochester, New York

69. ROBERT HOWLETT
Isambard Kingdom Brunel
c. 1857
Albumen prints of collodion negatives
Stereo; arched top of each image 7.1 × 7.1 cm
Jonathan Steel, United Kingdom
Note: No. 16 of the series 'The Great Eastern in the
Stereoscope'

70. ROBERT HOWLETT
'The Leviathan' steam ship
c. 1857
Albumen prints of collodion negatives
Stereo; each image 7.0 × 7.3 cm
Brian May, United Kingdom
Note: 'View showing drum and big chains and position of
ship before commencement of launch. Photographed by
Robert Howlett and George Downes. Published by the
Photographic Institution, 168 New Bond Street' (from
printed label on verso).

JOHN DILLWYN LLEWELYN 1810-1887

Llewelyn, whose wife was a cousin of Fox Talbot, the inventor
of the paper negative-positive process, began experimenting with
photography in 1839. He worked with many processes, including
daguerreotypes, and invented his own "dry" collodion — the
oxymel process. A gentleman of independent means, Llewelyn
lived on an estate in South Wales, Penllergare, which provided
him with subjects for many pictures. The plants and stuffed
animals and birds in his pictures are evidence of his interest in
botany and natural history, and some of his coastal scenes reflect
his study of geology. Thereza Llewelyn shared her father's
scientific interests. Llewelyn's motion studies, "instantaneous"
pictures of waves, smoke, etc., were admired at the time.

71. J. D. LLEWELYN
Piscator, No. 2
From: *Photographic Album for the Year 1857*, no. 20
1856
Lightly albumenized print of oxymel (collodion) negative
("Oxymel, June 1856, weather dull, exposure 20 minutes,

developed in pyrogallic acid. Lens by Ross, focal length 23″,
diameter 4″, diaphragm ½″″)
24.1 × 19.0 cm
International Museum of Photography at George Eastman
House, Rochester, New York

72. J. D. LLEWELYN
The Garden (Conservatory at Penllergare)
c. mid 1850s
Salted paper print of collodion negative
20.8 × 15.6 cm
National Gallery of Canada, Ottawa

73. J. D. LLEWELYN
Gypsies (the artist's children)
c. early 1850s
Salted paper print of paper negative
15.8 × 21.6 cm
International Museum of Photography at George Eastman
House, Rochester, New York

74. J. D. LLEWELYN
Rustic Well
c. early 1850s
Salted paper print of paper negative
20.6 × 25.7 cm
Royal Photographic Society, Bath

75. J. D. LLEWELYN
(A Rocky Coastal Scene)
c. mid 1850s
Salted paper print of collodion negative
25.1 × 20.2 cm
Royal Photographic Society, Bath

76. J. D. LLEWELYN
A Stag, An Otter, Pheasants, A Rabbit
c. mid 1850s
Albumen prints of collodion negatives
Ovals, approximately 16 × 20 cm
Royal Photographic Society, Bath
Note: It was a common practice in the 1850s to exhibit many
photographs in the same frame

77. J. D. LLEWELYN
Crawley Rocks, Oxwich Bay, Glamorganshire
c. 1853
Wood engraving after print from collodion negative
15 × 22.2 cm
From: *Illustrated London News*, 26, 14 April 1855, p. 349
Victoria and Albert Museum, London
Note: This view, which Llewelyn contributed to the
Photographic Exchange Club in 1855 or 1856, is one of his
"motion studies".

78. J. D. LLEWELYN
Portrait of Thereza Llewelyn Surrounded by a Photogram
of Seaweed
c. mid 1850s
Albumen print of collodion negative
23.5 × 18.6 cm
Metropolitan Museum of Art, New York

79. THEREZA LLEWELYN (1834-c1920s)
Album containing photogenic drawings of seaweed
c. 1853
23 × 20 cm
Private collection, United Kingdom

R. W. S. Lutwidge was Commissioner in Lunacy. As an
enthusiastic amateur photographer he introduced his nephew,
Charles Lutwidge Dodgson (Lewis Carroll) to the art.

80. R. S. W. LUTWIDGE
St. Michael's Mount, Cornwall
Photographic Exchange Club print, 1857-8 exchange
c. mid 1850s
Lightly albumenized print of paper negative
15.8 × 19.8 cm
Norfolk Record Office, Norwich, Eaton collection

81. R. W. S. LUTWIDGE
Still Life and Embroidery
From: *Photographic Album for the Year 1857*, no. 21
1856
Albumen print of collodion negative ("Taken on collodion
November 1856, weather dull, exposure 3 minutes,
developed by pyrogallic acid. Lens by Lerebour and
Secretan, focal length 14″, diameter 2¾″, diaphragm ½″.
Printed on albumenized paper by a friend.")
15.8 × 18.5 cm
Royal Photographic Society, Bath

In 1861 Mary Lynn was recorded as living with her brother, Lt.
Colonel James Lynn, then retired from the Royal Engineers.
Since members of this branch of the service had been given
instruction in photography for use in recording constructing and
copying maps, it may have been her brother who introduced her
to photography.

82. MARY LYNN
Lane Scene at Petistree, Suffolk
From: *Photographic Album for the Year 1855*
1855
Lightly albumenized print of collodion negative
("Collodion, Sept. 19, 1855, alternate clouds and sunshine,
exposure two minutes, developed with pyrogallic acid, lens
by A. Ross, focal length 12″, diameter 2½″, diaphragm 1/16″)
Oval 15.1 × 20.1 cm
Royal Photographic Society, Bath

83. MARY LYNN
Parnham Hall, Suffolk
c. mid 1850s
Albumen print of collodion negative
15.3 × 20.5 cm
International Museum of Photography at George Eastman
House, Rochester, New York
Note: annotated on mount: "collodion Ponham [sic] Hall,
Suffolk,
Photo Mary Lynn; on verso: W. C. 1858"

According to his obituary, Mackinlay "although in business . . .
devoted a considerable amount of his time to scientific pursuits,
and was possessed of means which enabled him to liberally
gratify his refined tastes." He began photographing in the early
1840s.

84. THOMAS G. MACKINLAY
Study for a Picture
From: *Photographic Album for the Year 1857*, no. 25

1856
Albumen print of collodion negative ("Taken on collodion,
June 1856, weather fine, exposure half a minute, developed
by a friend in Pyrogallic acid. Lens by Ross, focal length 12″,
diameter 2½″, diaphragm ⅝″. Printed on albumenized paper
by a friend.")
16.0 × 19.4 cm
International Museum of Photography at George Eastman
House, Rochester, New York

JOHN RICHARDSON MAJOR 1797-1876 or 1821-1871

The Reverend J. R. Major was Headmaster of King's College
School, where his son, also Rev. J. R. Major, was an assistant
master. King's College, where Delamotte taught drawing and
photography and Hardwich experimented with photographic
chemistry, was a centre of early photographic activity. Both J.
R. Majors were photographers, both were members of the
Photographic Society Club, and both had antiquarian interests.
it is not always possible to distinguish their photographs.
85. J. R. MAJOR
     Newark Abbey, near Chertsey
     From: *Photographic Album for the Year 1857*, no. 22
     1856
     Lightly albumenized print of paper negative ("Taken by the
     calotype process July 17, 1856 in sunshine. Exposure 4½
     minutes, developed with nitrate of silver and gallic acid.
     Lens by Gaudin, Paris, focal length 16½″, diameter 3″,
     diaphragm ½″. Printed in the ordinary method toned with
     gold by Mr. Hardwich, King's College")
     16.5 × 12.7 cm
     International Museum of Photography at George Eastman
     House, Rochester, New York
86. J. R. MAJOR
     Durley Manor House, Hants.
     Photographic Exchange Club print, 1857 exchange
     c. mid 1850s
     Albumen print of paper negative
     17.6 × 22.0 cm
     Royal Photographic Society, Bath

THOMAS LUKIS MANSELL 1809-1879

Dr. Mansell was a physician and Jurat who lived on Guernsey. In
the early 1850s he was an avid experimenter with calotype
processes and suggested a table of "Photographic Experience" by
which amateurs could compare exposure times, processes and
equipment. By the mid 1850s he had switched to collodion and
was especially interested in "dry" or syruped collodion.
87. T. L. MANSELL
     Lane, Guernsey
     Photographic Exchange Club print, 1855
     1855
     Albumen print of syruped collodion negative
     Oval 24.7 × 20.8 cm
     International Museum of Photography at George Eastman
     House, Rochester, New York
     Note: annotated on verso: "Canson Neg. Apl. 7 55 TLM,"
     and on mount, recto: "collodion c. Syr Lane Guernsey T. L.
     Mansell 1855"

88. T. L. MANSELL
     Fountain, Sark
     Photographic Exchange Club print, 1855-6
     c. 1855
     Albumen print of collodion negative
     18.6 × 23.7 cm
     Robert Hershkowitz, London
89. T. L. MANSELL
     Harbour, St. Peter's Port, Guernsey
     Photographic Exchange Club print, 1857-8 exchange
     c. mid 1850s
     Lightly albumenized print of syruped collodion negative
     17.1 × 22.4 cm
     Norfolk Record Office, Norwich, Eaton collection
90. T. L. MANSELL
     Highland Cottage, Village of Ardnaherra, Loch Fine,
     Argyleshire
     From: *Photographic Album for the year 1855*, no. 44
     1854
     Lightly albumenized print of collodion negative ("Collodion,
     July 1854, diffused light exposed 45 seconds, developed in
     pyrogallic acid. Lens by Slater, focal length 17″, diameter
     3¼″, diaphragm ½″")
     16.5 × 21.0 cm
     Royal Photographic Society, Bath
91. T. L. MANSELL
     Port de Dinan, Brittany
     From: *Photographic Album for the Year 1857*, no. 24
     1856
     Lightly albumenized print of syruped collodion negative
     ("Taken on syruped collodion 6 AM June 28, 1856, in bright
     sunshine, exposure 47 minutes, developed by pyrogallic
     acid. Lens by Ross, focal length 12½″, diameter 2½″,
     diaphragm ⅝″, printed with the Sel d'Or process by T. L.
     Mansell")
     21.8 × 26.8 cm
     International Museum of Photography at George Eastman
     House, Rochester, New York

COUNT DE MONTIZON active 1850s

A London member of the Photographic Society, the Count de
Montizon lived in Brompton. He belonged to the group
surrounding Dr. Diamond, and appears in one of Diamond's
photographs, standing on the steps of the Asylum. In 1853 he
read a paper on the collodion process before the Photographic
Society in which he told how to prepare collodion and discussed
the possibility of arresting momentary movements of birds.
92. COUNT DE MONTIZON
     The Hippopotamus at the Zoological Gardens, Regent's Park.
     From: *Photographic Album for the Year 1855*, no. 9
     1855
     Albumen print of collodion negative ("Taken on collodion
     with a double lens, instantaneous exposure.")
     11.2 × 12.7 cm
     Royal Photographic Society, Bath
93. COUNT DE MONTIZON
     Camel
     c. mid 1850s
     Lightly albumenized print of collodion negative
     11.4 × 10.1 cm

International Museum of Photography at George Eastman
House, Rochester, New York
94. COUNT DE MONTIZON
A Pike
c. mid 1850s
Lightly albumenized print of collodion negative
8.6 × 9.6 cm
International Museum of Photography at George Eastman
House, Rochester, New York

LADY AUGUSTA MOSTYN 1830-1912

A member of an aristocratic family, Lady Augusta, along with
her sisters, Ladies Caroline and Isabel Nevill, adventurously
took up photography in the 1850s. Her exchange club albums are
in the collection of International Museum of Photography at
George Eastman House. As a young widow, she was responsible
for the development of the resort of Llandudno in North Wales
— part of her husband's estate.
95. LADY AUGUSTA MOSTYN
Malling Abbey, Kent
Photographic Exchange Club print, 1855-6 exchange
c. mid 1850s
Albumen print of waxed paper negative
18.0 × 20.4 cm
International Museum of Photography at George Eastman
House, Rochester, New York
96. LADY AUGUSTA MOSTYN
Oak Tree in Eridge Park, Sussex
Photographic Exchange Club print, 1857-8 exchange
c. mid 1850s
Albumen(?) print of waxed paper(?) negative
17.5 × 19.2 cm
International Museum of Photography at George Eastman
House, Rochester, New York
97. LADY AUGUSTA MOSTYN
Path through Ruins
c. mid 1850s
Salted paper print of waxed paper negative
17.1 × 20.0 cm
Marian King, United Kingdom
98. LADY AUGUSTA MOSTYN
Trees against a Rocky Outcrop
c. mid 1850s
Salted paper print of waxed paper negative
17.8 × 23.0 cm
Marian King, United Kingdom
99. LADY AUGUSTA MOSTYN
Stone Wall and Trees
c. mid 1850s
Albumen print of paper negative
12.1 × 15.6 cm
Marian King, United Kingdom
100. LADY AUGUSTA MOSTYN
Eridge Green, Sussex
Photographic Exchange Club print, 1857 exchange
c. mid 1850s
Albumen print of waxed paper negative
18.4 × 20.3 cm
Royal Photographic Society, Bath
Note: These cottages, opposite the entrance to Eridge

Park, the Nevill's seat, were built by the second Earl of
Abergavenny, the grandfather of the photographer, as
housing for his workers.

LADY CAROLINE NEVILL 1829-1887

Like her sister Lady Augusta Mostyn, Lady Caroline Nevill
photographed scenes in and near the family estates especially
Eridge Park near Tonbridge Wells. Photographs of family
members and events pasted into albums are reported to have
been taken and compiled by Lady Caroline. A critic wrote of
works exhibited in the 1852 exhibition: "The amateur productions
of the Ladies Neville [sic], groups and portraits, pleasantly
report to us some of the improved employment of their leisure by
some members of the aristocracy of the present day."
101. LADY CAROLINE NEVILL
Birling, Kent
Photographic Exchange Club print, 1857-8 exchange
c. mid 1850s
Salted paper print of waxed paper negative
13.1 × 20.1 cm
International Museum of Photography at George Eastman
House, Rochester, New York
102. LADY CAROLINE NEVILL
Allington Castle
Photographic Exchange Club print, 1855-6 exchange
c. mid 1850s
Albumen print of waxed paper negative
18.0 × 20.8 cm
International Museum of Photography at George Eastman
House, Rochester, New York
103. LADY CAROLINE NEVILL
The Trio (Isabel, Caroline and Augusta Nevill)
c. early 1850s
Lightly albumenized print of paper negative
10.1 × 9.0 cm
Mrs. Norman Wingfield-Stratford Johnstone, United
Kingdom
104. LADY CAROLINE NEVILL
Woman (Lady Caroline) with a Dog
c. early 1850s
Lightly albumenized print of collodion negative
10.0 × 8.0 cm
Mrs. Norman Wingfield-Stratford Johnstone, United
Kingdom
Note: The pictures in this album were attributed to Lady
Caroline by Esme Wingfield-Stratford in a biography of his
grandfather, Lady Isabel Nevill's husband, *This Was a Man*.
Since this picture shows Lady Caroline, it is likely that it
was taken by one of her sisters.
105. LADY CAROLINE NEVILL
Woman Asleep on a Sofa (Lady Augusta)
c. mid 1850s
Lightly albumenized print of collodion negative
7.0 × 8.5 cm
Mrs. Norman Wingfield-Stratford Johnstone, United
Kingdom

Sir William Newton was a popular miniature painter and a member of the Royal Academy. He was one of the founders of the Photographic Society, and at its first meeting created a stir by suggesting that sharp focus was not necessarily true to artistic experience. Despite his professional interest in portraiture, his surviving photographs are all of landscape and architecture.

106. SIR WILLIAM J. NEWTON
    Burnham Beeches
    Photographic Exchange Club print, 1855-56 exchange
    c. mid 1850s
    Salted paper print of calotype negative
    17.0 × 22.3 cm
    Royal Photographic Society, Bath
    Note: Two frames each of six views of Burnham Beeches
    were exhibited by Sir William Newton at the first exhibition
    of the Photographic Society of London in 1854.
107. SIR WILLIAM J. NEWTON [attributed to]
    Burnham Beeches
    c. mid 1850s
    Albumen print of paper negative
    17.5 × 20.0 cm
    King's College, London
108. SIR WILLIAM J. NEWTON [attributed to]
    Burnham Beeches
    c. mid 1850s
    Lightly albumenized print of paper negative
    17.3 × 20.9 cm
    King's College, London

W. H. Nicholl was member of the Photographic Society who lived in Usk, Monmouthshire in South Wales.

109. W. H. NICHOLL
    Crwmlyn Viaduct, Monmouthshire
    From: *Photographic Album for the Year 1855*, no. 41
    1854
    Albumen print of collodion negative ("Taken on collodion in
    Archer's camera 8 August 1854, with bright sun and clouds
    in the background. Exposed 1½ minutes. Developed with
    pyrogallic acid. Lens by Archer, focal length 16", diameter 3",
    diaphragm ½".")
    21.2 × 18.7 cm
    Royal Photographic Society, Bath
110. W.H. NICHOLL
    Windsor Park, Deer Feeding
    From: *Photographic Album for the Year 1857*
    1854
    Lightly albumenized print of collodion negative ("Taken on
    collodion May 1854, weather rather foggy, exposure 2
    minutes, developed by pyrogallic acid. Lens by Goddard,
    focal length 13", diameter 3¼", diaphragm ¾", printed in
    the ordinary way by W. H. N.")
    15.0 × 21.1 cm
    International Museum of Photography at George Eastman
    House, Rochester, New York

A medical education was one of the few ways to receive training in science in the middle of the nineteenth century. Dr. Percy did not practice medicine, but did research in metallurgy and related fields. The chemistry of photography attracted him in the 1840s; in the 1850s he turned to making picturesque landscapes. Later he gave up photography and collected water-colours – he gave the catalogue of his collection to the British Museum.

111. JOHN PERCY
    Cedar at Kew
    Photographic Exchange Club Print, 1855-6 exchange
    c. mid 1850s
    Albumen print of paper negative
    28.5 × 21.0 cm
    International Museum of Photography at George Eastman
    House, Rochester, New York
112. JOHN PERCY and JOHN SPILLER
    The New Mill, Near Lynton, North Devon
    From: *Photographic Album for the Year 1857*, no. 28
    1856
    Albumen print of collodion negative ("Taken on collodion at
    the end of September 1856 in feeble not continuous sunshine,
    exposed about eight minutes, with the mill being entirely in
    shadow, developed by pyrogallic acid. The lens was focused
    on the wheel. Printed and toned with gold by Mr. Hardwich,
    Kings College. Lens by Ross, focal length 18", diameter 3½",
    diaphragm ⅝".")
    30.2 × 23.6
    International Museum of Photography at George Eastman
    House, Rochester, New York
113. JOHN PERCY
    View out a Window
    c. mid 1850s
    Albumen print of collodion negative
    Wheatstone stereo, each image: 21.3 × 18.3 cm
    King's College, London, Wheatstone collection

Julius Pollock was a half-brother of Henry. He was educated at King's College, London, and received an M.D. from St. Andrews in 1861. In addition to landscapes, he photographed tableaux and documented the appearance of people with deformities.

114. A. J. POLLOCK
    (Photographs of people with deformities)
    From: album, Royal Medical and Chiurgical Society
    Photographs. B. Surgical
    c. mid 1850s
    Albumen prints of collodion negatives
    Album: 67.6 × 52.7 cm
    Royal College of Medicine, London

Henry and Alfred Julius Pollock were two of the twenty children (by two wives) of the Rt. Hon. Sir Frederick Pollock, Lord Chief Baron of the Exchequer, who was also a photographer and the second president of the Photographic Society.

115. HENRY POLLOCK
After Luncheon
Photographic Exchange Club print, 1857 exchange
c. mid 1850s
Albumen print of collodion negative
13.1 × 30.5 cm
Royal Photographic Society, Bath
116. HENRY POLLOCK
The Mouth of the East and West Lyn, Lynmouth, North
Devon
From: *Photographic Album for the Year 1857*, no. 27
1856
Albumen print of collodion negative ("Taken on collodion
(wet) August 1856, weather rainy, exposure 3 minutes,
developed in pyrogallic acid (one grain to the ounce). Lens
by ross, focal length 24″, diameter 4″, diaphragm ½″. Printed
on ordinary albumenized paper, toned with gold by H. P.")
30.2 × 23.6 cm
Royal Photographic Society, Bath

WILLIAM LAKE PRICE c. 1810-1896

Lake Price began his career as an artist and illustrator of
books. He exhibited pictures regularly at the Royal Academy
between 1828 and 1832 and at the Royal Watercolour Society
between 1828 and 1852. During the 1850s his posed narrative
photographs, which drew upon his past experience, were hailed
as being "of an entirely new character" and "marked by great
artistic feeling." They achieved success as stereos as well as in
larger formats. Price's *Manual of Photographic Manipulation*,
1858, was the first book to combine practical technical advice
with artistic instruction. In 1862, pleading ill-health, he gave up
his career as a photographer.

117. LAKE PRICE
An Interior
Photographic Exchange Club print, 1855-6 exchange
c. 1855
Albumen print of collodion negative
17.4 × 17.4 cm
International Museum of Photography at George Eastman
House, Rochester, New York
118. LAKE PRICE
The Miniature
From: *Photographic Album for the Year 1855*, no. 14
1855
Albumen print of collodion negative ("Collodion, June 1855,
weather fine, exposure 10 seconds, developed by pyrogallic
acid. Lens by Ross, focal length 15″, diameter 4½″,
diaphragm 3″.")
Oval 22.2 × 18.4 cm
Royal Photographic Society, Bath
119. LAKE PRICE
Don Quixote in his Study
From: *Photographic Art Treasures*, part II
1857
Photogalvanographic print
31.9 × 27.9 cm
Metropolitan Museum of Art, New York
Note: This popular image was also issued as a photographic
print and stereo. For The Bradford showing the volume of
Photographic Art Treasures will be lent from the collection of
the Central Library, Manchester

120. LAKE PRICE
A Brace of Birds
From: *Photographic Art Treasures*, parts IV and V
1857
Photogalvanographic print
Arched top: 29.4 × 24.7 cm
Royal Photographic Society, Bath
121. LAKE PRICE
Caterina Cornaro's Chamber
From: *Interiors and Exteriors in Venice*, lithographed by
Joseph Nash
from the Original Drawings, London, T. McLean, 1843, pl.
c. 1843
Lithograph
29.6 × 42.5 cm
International Museum of Photography at George Eastman
House, Rochester, New York
122. LAKE PRICE
Don Quixote
1857
Albumen prints of collodion negatives
Stereo: each image 7.0 × 7.0 cm
Russell Norton, New Haven
123. LAKE PRICE
Robinson Crusoe and Friday
1857
Albumen prints of collodion negatives, hand coloured
Stereo: each image 7.9 × 7.5 cm
Russell Norton, New Haven
124. LAKE PRICE
Robinson Crusoe and Friday
1857
Albumen prints of collodion negatives, hand coloured
Stereo: each image 7.9 × 7.7 cm
Russell Norton, New Haven

WILLIAM HARCOURT RANKING active 1850s

Dr. Ranking was educated at Cambridge and later licensed in
medicine. He was Senior Physician at Norwich and edited the
Half-Yearly Abstract of the Medical Sciences and the *Provincial
Medical and Surgical Journal*. His letters to the *Journal of the
Photographic Society* attest to his interest in the chemistry of
photography.

125. DR. RANKING
Church Porch, Earlham, near Norwich
From: *Photographic Album for the Year 1857*, no. 31
c. 1857
Albumen print of wax paper negative ("Taken by
Sedgefield's wax paper process in the month of April in
medium sunshine. Exposure 17 minutes, developed in a
saturated solution of gallic acid in aceto nitrate. Lens by
Ross, focal length 21″, diameter 3¼″, diaphragm ½″. Printed
on albumen paper toned with chloride of gold by
Dr. Ranking.")
25.4 × 20.2 cm
International Museum of Photography at George Eastman
House, Rochester, New York

Rejlander was famous for his narrative photographs made by combination printing, and he became a successful art photographer. His most famous and controversial picture, *Two Ways of Life* (1857), became acceptable to the public after a copy was purchased by Queen Victoria for Prince Albert. Rejlander's participation in the exchange within the Photographic Society shows his ties with amateur photography in the mid 1850s.

126. O. G. REJLANDER
Fortune Telling
From: *Photographic Album for the year 1855*, no. 24
1855
Albumen print of collodion negative ("Collodion, August 30, 1855, clear with clouds floating before the sun. Exposure 11 seconds, developed with pyrogallic acid. Lens, by Ross focal length 15″, diameter 3″, diaphragm 1″.")
19.6 × 16.0 cm
Royal Photographic Society, Bath

HENRY PEACH ROBINSON 1830-1901

Robinson had artistic training before he became interested in photography. He was a protege of Dr. Diamond, who introduced him into the Photographic Exchange Club and encouraged him to become a new kind of professional photographer — one who did not depend upon portraits. During the mid 1850s, Robinson shared the picturesque subjects of amateur photographers, but also began making narrative pictures and combination prints from several negatives. When *Fading Away* became an instant success in 1858, he was launched as a photographer who promoted art, both in his pictures and his very successful manuals.

127. H. P. ROBINSON
Guy's Cliffe, Warwickshire
Photographic Exchange Club print, 1857 exchange
c. 1857
Albumen print of collodion negative
15.5 × 20.4 cm
International Museum of Photography at George Eastman House, Rochester, New York
Note: In Robinson's album, in the collection of the Royal Photographic Society, this print is annotated: "my first landscape, taken at 6:20 AM"

128. H. P. ROBINSON
On the Avon, Stoneleigh
Photographic Exchange Club print, 1858 exchange
c. 1857
Albumen print of collodion negative
18.8 × 24.1 cm
Royal Photographic Society, Bath
Note: In the Mostyn album, in the collection of the International Museum of Photography at George Eastman House, this print is annotated: "Exposed 3 minutes"

129. H. P. ROBINSON
Going a Milking
Amateur Photographic Association print
c. 1859
Albumen print of collodion negative
20.4 × 15.3 cm; vignetted image 15.0 × 11.5 cm
International Museum of Photography at George Eastman House, Rochester, New York

130. H. P. ROBINSON
Four carte de visites
early 1860s
Albumen prints of collodion negatives
Each image approximately 9.0 × 5.6 cm
Jonathan Steel, United Kingdom

131. H. P. ROBINSON
(Two girls)
From: H. P. Robinson, *Pictorial Effect in Photography*, London, Piper & Carter, 1869
c. 1860s
Carbon print of collodion negative
11.5 × 9.0 cm
International Museum of Photography at George Eastman House, Rochester, New York

ALFRED ROSLING 1802-1880s

Rosling was a successful timber merchant who took an interest in the financial affairs of photographic institutions; he was the first Treasurer of the Photographic Society. He began photographing in the 1840s and experimented with micro-photographs; he also made reductions of pages of the *Illustrated London News*. Most of his photographs are picturesque landscapes. He lived next door to his son-in-law, Francis Frith, who later included prints from some of Rosling's negatives among the pictures he published for sale.

132. ALFRED ROSLING
Scene near Godalming, Surrey
c. mid 1850s
Albumen print of collodion negative
15.3 × 20.1 cm
Art Institute of Chicago

133. ALFRED ROSLING
View in Betchworth Park, Surrey
negative c. mid 1850s, printed in the 1860s by Frith & Co.
Albumen print of collodion negative
20.8 × 17.1 cm
Victoria and Albert Museum

134. ALFRED ROSLING
Pass Near Nant Frangen, North Wales
Negative 1858, printed in the 1860s by Frith & Co.
Albumen print of collodion negative
16.7 × 21.3 cm
Private Collection, United Kingdom
Note: This photograph was no.34 in the *Photographic Album for the Year 1857*, "Taken on collodion, July 1858, weather stormy, exposure 2 minutes, developed by pyrogallic acid. Lens by Ross, focal length 12″, diameter 2½″, diaphragm ¼″. Printed in the ordinary way by Alfred Rosling."

135. ALFRED ROSLING
Conway Castle
c. mid 1850s
Albumen print of collodion negative
11.6 × 20.9 cm
Philippe Garner, London
Note: Rosling contributed an alternative view of Conway Castle to the Photographic Exchange Club in 1858

136. ALFRED ROSLING
Ransomes & Sims 12 Horse Power Fixed Gothic Steam Engine

1854
Albumen prints of collodion negatives
Stereo: ovals each image 7.2 × 6.2 cm
Russell Norton, New Haven
Note: annotated on verso: "Negative by A. Rosling 5 March
1854"

137. ALFRED ROSLING
Ransomes & Sims 6 Horse Power Portable Steam Engine
1854
Albumen prints of collodion negatives
Stereo: ovals each image 7.2 × 6.2 cm
Russell Norton, New Haven
Note: annotated on verso: "Negative by A. Rosling 5 March
1854"

GEORGE SHADBOLT 1819-1901

A merchant who sold fine wool, Shadbolt lived in Hornsey.
Although it would soon be transformed into a suburb of London,
he documented its rural aspects and hand industry. He was
knowledgeable about lenses and interested in microscopy; he
studied algae and produced tiny photographs for examination in
microscopes. He edited the *Liverpool and Manchester
Photographic Journal*, which became the *British Journal of
Photography*, from 1857 to 1864.

138. GEORGE SHADBOLT
The High Gate
c. mid 1850s
Salted paper print of collodion negative
16.5 × 22.9 cm
Bruce Castle Museum, London

139. GEORGE SHADBOLT
The Morning Ramble
c. mid 1850s
Salted paper print of collodion negative
23.1 × 18.0 cm
Bruce Castle Museum, London
Note: Inscribed on verso: "Bridge from Middle Lane to
Priory Road, Hornsey"

140. GEORGE SHADBOLT
Handmade Brick Puddling
c. mid 1850s
Salted paper print of collodion negative
17.2 × 21.5 cm
Bruce Castle Museum, London
Note: At a time of rapid building, Shadbolt chose to show an
old-fashioned hand process.

141. GEORGE SHADBOLT
Looking over the Vale of Hornsey
c. mid 1850s
Salted paper print of collodion negative
17.0 × 22.2 cm
Bruce Castle Museum, London

142. GEORGE SHADBOLT
The Laundress's Cottage
Photographic Exchange Club print, 1857 exchange
c. mid 1850s
Salted paper print of collodion negative
17.0 × 20.4 cm
Bruce Castle Museum, London

143. GEORGE SHADBOLT

Top of Hornsey Rise
c. mid 1850s
Salted paper print of collodion negative
16.8 × 21.4 cm
Bruce Castle Museum, London

144. GEORGE SHADBOLT
Priory Road, Hornsey
c. mid 1850s
Salted paper print of collodion negative
17.8 × 22.0 cm
Bruce Castle Museum, London

145. GEORGE SHADBOLT
View in Mt. Pleasant Fields, Hornsey
Amateur Photographic Association print
c. late 1850s
Albumen print of collodion negative
16.1 × 20.5 cm
International Museum of Photography at George Eastman
House, Rochester, New York

GEORGE B. STOKES active 1850s

A London member of the Photographic Society, George Stokes
lived in Bayswater. His contributions to both of the
Photographic Albums were views of Tenby.

146. GEORGE B. STOKES
Tenby Harbour, South Wales
From: *Photographic Album for the Year 1855*, no. 5
1853
Albumen print of collodion negative ("Collodion, October
1853, sunny morning, exposure 40 seconds, developed with
pyrogallic acid. Lens by Voigtlander, focal length 7½",
diameter 3½", diaphragm ½".")
19.0 × 15.3 cm
Royal Photographic Society, Bath

WILLIAM JOHN THOMS 1803-1885

An antiquary and man of letters, Thoms founded and edited
the journal *Notes and Queries*. During the early 1850s it was an
important medium for the exchange of information on
photography.

147. WILLIAM J. THOMS
The Very Old Oak, Windsor
Photographic Exchange Club print, 1857 exchange
c. mid 1850s
Lightly albumenized print of paper negative
16.0 × 19.7 cm
Royal Photographic Society, Bath

148. WILLIAM J. THOMS
Herne's Oak, Windsor
Photographic Exchange Club print, 1858 exchange
c. mid 1850s
Salted paper print of paper negative
15.4 × 19.7 cm
Royal Photographic Society, Bath

BENJAMIN BRECKNELL TURNER 1815-1894

B. B. Turner was a successful tallow chandler. He began
photographing in 1849. Between 1852 and 1854 he took many

views on paper negatives of scenes in Worcestershire, especially in and near Bredicot, where his brother-in-law was a gentleman farmer. Turner persisted in showing prints from paper negatives after many of his contemporaries had turned to collodion.

149. B. B. TURNER
Old Doorway, Pershore Abbey
1852-54
26.3 × 38.9 cm
Albumen print of paper negative
Victoria and Albert Museum, London

150. B. B. TURNER
Hedgerow Trees, Clerkenleap, Worcestershire
1852-4
Albumen print of paper negative
26.5 × 37.3 cm
Victoria and Albert Museum, London

151. B. B. TURNER
Hawkhurst Church, Kent
c. 1852
Albumen print of paper negative
26.1 × 36.1 cm
Victoria and Albert Museum, London
Note: according to Turner's son this was exhibited in 1852 with the title *Photographic Truth*.

152. B. B. TURNER
Foldyard, Bredicot
1852-4
Albumen print of paper negative
26.2 × 38.0 cm
Victoria and Albert Museum, London

153. B. B. TURNER
Hurtmore Lane, Surrey
1852-4
Albumen print of paper negative
26.1 × 38.4 cm
Victoria and Albert Museum, London

154. B. B. TURNER
View of the Lyn
1852-4
Albumen print of paper negative
26.9 × 39.1 cm
Victoria and Albert Museum, London

HENRY WHITE 1819-1903

Henry White was admitted to the Roll of Solicitors in 1841 and practised law with his father, Richard Samuel White, as White and Son. After his father's death in 1857, White continued his practice from a different Bloomsbury address. In 1856 he published a series of landscape photographs mounted on heavy paper with dated letterpress inscriptions: "London, Photographed & Published by Henry White," While these seem to have been intended for sale, he remained an amateur photographer and, like many of his colleagues, seems to have stopped photographing around 1860.

155. HENRY WHITE
The Garden Chair
From: *Photographic Album for the Year 1855*, no. 11
1854
Albumen print of collodion negative ("Taken on collodion September 11, 1854, about 1 PM in fine sunshine, exposed 5 seconds, developed in pyrogallic acid. Lens by Ross, focal length 10″, diameter 3″, double lens, diameter 3‴″)
17.8 × 14 cm
Royal Photographic Society, Bath

156. HENRY WHITE
Hunford Mill, Surrey
c. mid 1850s
Albumen print of collodion negative
19.3 × 23.8 cm
Daniel Wolf, Inc., New York

157. HENRY WHITE
Falls on the Llugwy nr. Bettws-y-Coed
c. mid 1850s
Albumen print of collodion negative
24.9 × 20.0 cm
Daniel Wolf, Inc., New York

158. HENRY WHITE
Old Cottage at Chertsey Lane End
c. mid 1850s
Albumen print of collodion negative
19.6 × 24.9 cm
Robert Hershkowitz, London

159. HENRY WHITE
Mill at Weybridge
c. mid 1850s
Albumen print of collodion negative
19.9 × 24.5 cm
Robert Hershkowitz, London

SUPPORTING MATERIAL

160. PHOTOGRAPHIC ART TREASURES
Wrapper
Photogalvanographic print by Fenton(?)
55.6 × 38.0 cm
Royal Photographic Society, Bath

161. WILLIAM WESTALL
Melrose Abbey, Scotland
From: William Westall, *The Landscape Album or Great Britain Illustrated*, London, Charles Tilt, 1832, frontispiece
c. 1830
Engraving
12.7 × 9.7 cm
Rush Rhees Library, University of Rochester

162. UNIDENTIFIED ARTIST
Sentiment/Remembrance Album owned by Marion Olliver
c. mid 1850s
Rush Rhees Library, University of Rochester

163. UNIDENTIFIED ARTIST
Sentiment/Remembrance Album owned by Harriet Anne Cockerell
c. 1820s-1830s
Rush Rhees Library, University of Rochester

164. MYLES BIRKET FOSTER (1825-1899)
An Old English Mill
c. mid 19th century
Etching
25.0 × 17.7 cm (image) 31.2 × 24.6 cm (sheet)
Private collector, United States
Note: see Percy's, New Mill, near Lynton, North Devon

165. S. C. JONES and L. HAGHE (drawn by Jones, lithographed by
Haghe)
Interior View of West Window, Tintern Abbey
c. first half of 19th century
Lithograph
25.2 × 17.8 cm (image) 38.1 × 28.1 cm (page)
Private collector, United States
Note: see Delamotte's Brinkburn Priory, Rievaulx Abbey,
etc.
166. F. MACKENZIE and HENRY LE KEUX (drawn by Mackenzie,
engraved by Le Keux)
West View of the Erpingham Gate, *Cathedral Antiquities*,
pl. XXIII
1816
Engraving
21.8 × 14.7 cm (image), 27.0 × 20.0 cm (sheet)
Private collector, United States
Note: see Eaton's Erpingham Gate
167. W. WARD, AFTER SIR JOSHUA REYNOLDS
The Gypsy Fortune Teller
c. 1800
Mezzotint
16.8 × 20.3 cm
Private collector, United States
Note: see Rejlander's Fortune Telling and copies of works of
art
168. W. S. HOWITT (1765-1822)
Game, from *British Sports*
Etching, hand coloured
11.6 × 18.0 cm (plate) 14.2 × 23.3 cm (sheet)
Private collector, United States
Note: see still life photographs by Lutwidge, Fenton,
Mackinlay
169. THE SUNBEAM
ed. Philip H. Delamotte
1857-1859
Royal Photographic Society, Bath

Library, Manchester; King's College, London; the
Metropolitan Museum of Art, New York; the Norfolk
Central Library and the Norfolk Records Office,
Norwich; Royal College of Medicine, London; the Royal
Photographic Society, Bath; Rush Rhees Library of the
University of Rochester; and the Society of Antiquaries,
London. Philippe Garner, Robert Hershkowitz, Harrison
Horblit, Mrs. Norman Wingfield-Stratford Johnstone,
Marian King, Brian May, Russell Norton, Sean Sexton,
Jonathan Steel, Paul Walter, Stephen White and Daniel
Wolf have all graciously consented to lend photographs
from their collections.

In addition the curators of the exhibition wish to
extend their thanks to the curators of the International
Museum of Photography at George Eastman House,
Robert Sobieszek and Janet Buerger, and Mark
Haworth-Booth, Christopher Titterington and Jennifer
Blain of the Victoria and Albert Museum, who helped to
coordinate the exhibition, and to Andrew Dempsey,
Assistant Director of Exhibitions (London), of the Arts
Council. Many others provided assistance and advice; we
should especially like to thank Richard Bloore, Stephanie
Frontz, Professor Margaret
Harker, Mary Huth, Valerie
Lloyd, Richard Morris, James
Reilly, Christopher Seiberling,
Alice Swan and Roger Taylor.
C. B. and G. S.

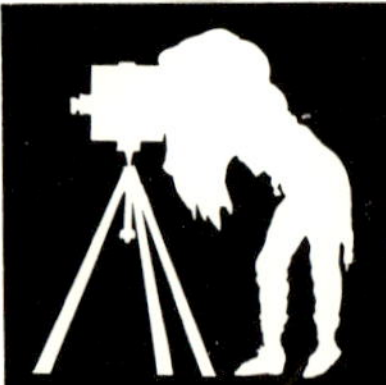

ACKNOWLEDGEMENTS

The exchanges of photographs among amateurs in
the 1850s, which were part of a remarkable
flowering of photography in that decade, are
fittingly presented here as the outcome of exchanges
between two countries. This exhibition is presented
under the joint sponsorship of the International Museum
of Photography at George Eastman House, the Arts
Council of Great Britain and the Victoria and Albert
Museum. It is supported by funds from the National
Endowment for the Arts, a Federal Agency, Washington,
and the New York State Council for the Arts as well as by
the Arts Council of Great Britain.

It is possible to show the Exchange Club prints
and others by these pioneering photographers through
the generosity of many lenders: The Art Institute of
Chicago; Bruce Castle Museum, London; The Central

The Museum is most grateful to the Greater London Council History
Library, the International Museum of Photography at George Eastham
House, the Royal College of Medicine, the Royal Photographic Society and
the Society of Antiquaries for permission to illustrate photographs from
their collections.